Did The Catholic Church Order Abraham Lincoln's Assassination?

James Battell

Published by James Battell, 2024.

DID THE CATHOLIC CHURCH ORDER ABRAHAM LINCOLN'S ASSASSINATION?

First edition. January 31, 2024.

ISBN: 979-8224476992

Written by James Battell.

Also by James Battell

The Shocking History of the Jesuits (The Society of Jesus)

King James I of England: The King The Vatican Could Not Kill

The Hidden Truth About Freemasonry, The Catholic Church, And The Illuminati

Bible Prophecy Made Simple For Serious Students of Scripture

Did The Catholic Church Order Abraham Lincoln's Assassination?

Is Calvinism And The Doctrines of Grace Biblical?

The Book of Genesis Commentary (Chapters 1-11)

Watchman Nee, Witness Lee, and Living Stream Ministry: A Critical Analysis of Their Identity as Cult or Church

What Is Speaking In Tongues And Is It Still For Today?

Ephesians Bible Commentary

The Book of Romans Commentary

Chapter 1: "Crimes And Conspiracies"

———

"**M**y concern is not whether God is on our side but my greatest concern is to be on God's side." A safe answer, it seems.

On Good Friday, April 14th 1865, Mrs Mary Todd Lincoln (by the way she is credited, it seems, to being referred to as the First Lady of the White House) persuaded her tired yet jubilant husband to attend the Ford's Theatre in Washington, where a popular comedy *Our American Cousin* was being performed that evening to an excited sell-out audience.

It might take his mind off the deeply bitter Civil War, she suggested to friends, as the play was finally coming to a conclusion. In fact, Mrs Lincoln had lost a half-brother fighting on the Confederate side and through spiritualism, dangerously attempted to communicate with him and her dead son, a wicked exercise to attempt.

(Incidentally, in 2008, the play would be adapted to create an opera).

Lincoln was then presiding over the final days of the torturous and terrible Civil War with the so-called "rebellious Confederate South," partly in retreat. Some historians of the Civil War period claim that Lincoln instigated the war himself. Now I'm not sure why, because the evidence is scant. Over

15,000 books have been written about him (can you believe?), 20% of them concerning the assassination. It seems that he is the most read subject in history, with the exception of Jesus Christ.

Some historians claim that his attempts to free the slaves (as we were always led to believe) had nothing to do with the popular misconception of the emancipation of the slaves, and that Lincoln was simply a petty tyrant and a war criminal according to some observers of the man, not to forget the inhumane treatment of civilians and captured soldiers in the Confederacy. There is some truth in some of these charges against him. An "American Stalin" was another accusing sobriquet used against him that I came across.

The gratifying news for this 16th American president days before that fateful visit to the theatre was that General Lee had finally surrendered his battle-weary troops in Virginia. Incidentally, General Lee's pre-war home and estate had been seized by marauding Union troops previously during the War, but today it is better known as the Arlington National Cemetery, and yes, the family were fully compensated, I'm informed.

However, many other Confederate generals in service were still very active in prolonging the War for whatever "patriotic" reasons they had. The Civil War seemed to have aged Lincoln, bringing with it sleepless nights and vivid dreams plus nightmares of ghostly white sail ships. No, this is not *Abraham Lincoln Vampire Hunter*, a popular kids' video game, if you did not know.

Fondly known by friends as "father Abraham or honest Abe," Lincoln agreed with his wife that an evening away at the theatre might be a pleasurable event, free from the pressures of the White House with all of its problems and nightly psychic occurrences. After all, he had not been sleeping too well. Many nights were broken, being plagued by nightmares and cold sweats and fears of the future. "Lincoln had always believed in and feared the power of dreams," recalled a friend years later.

After signing pressing presidential papers that momentous evening, the 16th president finally departed with his wife for the theatre, travelling as always in their usual horse and carriage and destined for an evening enjoyment, or so they hoped. He actually knew this theatre rather well, having in the past taken his young son Willy to watch performances and rehearsals, and always seated discreetly from the rear of the house stalls. Sadly, Willy would die of typhoid fever in the White House in 1862, then aged only eleven. Another son, Thomas, would die years later in 1871, possibly of tuberculosis. And his eldest son, Robert, then an officer serving in the Union Army, was on army leave that Good Friday, staying with his family in the White House. Apparently, he declined an invite by his mother to accompany both of them to the Ford Playhouse.

However, more suspicious to me is that General Grant and Secretary of War Edwin "Mars" Stanton, originally one of Lincoln's political foes and now the powerful Secretary of War, had once insulted Lincoln years before by calling him "that damned long-armed ape." Now, on that momentous evening, he had also declined the president's personal request to accompany Washington's first couple to the theatre, citing other urgent matters to attend to (more on Edwin Stanton in later chapters).

So, the president and first lady departed to take their waiting seats for an evening's entertainment, but President Abraham Lincoln will never return alive to the White House. Instead, he has an appointment with God, as one day we all will.

Never mind Lincoln! Are you ready to meet the Lord if your life is snuffed out like Lincoln's? Over 7,000 die each hour; it could soon be your turn. You need to think about this question very seriously!

Edwin P. Stanton, an American tsar

I was concerned when I read of Lincoln's family's frivolous flirtation with spiritualists because the Holy Bible condemns this evil practice many times, for example in Revelation 21:8, with many more Bible verses as well:

"But the fearful, and unbelieving, and the abominable, and murderers, and whoremongers, and sorcerers, and idolaters, and all liars, shall have their part in the lake which burneth with fire and brimstone: which is the second death."

If your favoured poison is tarot card readings, shaking chicken bones, looking at tea leaves, or experimenting with an Ouija board, then don't mess with them. And if you're into attending "spooky" séances on a wet afternoon, then get out of them all!! The road to Hell will be packed with people who played with this fire and burnt themselves, only to end up in the everlasting flames of Hell. You have been warned!

At 8.30 pm or 9.30 pm, Abraham with Mary and two invited guests, Major Henry Rathbone and his fiancée Clara Harris, entered the Ford vestibule. After a string rendition of "Hail to the Chief" from the orchestra pit, the Lincoln party settled into presidential box number 7, brightly prepared and festooned with flags and bunting and a fixed portrait of General Washington in pride of place on the balcony, no less.

That evening, the theatre was celebrating the one thousandth performance of *Our American Cousin*, starring the then-popular Miss Laura Keene. She later would offer a unique act of kindness to the dying president that will eclipse anything she ever attempted on the American stage in the past or would in the future at any American venue.

But, for now, an American tragedy was about to commence that evening, and the rest (as they say) is history.

On a personal note, some years ago I was researching the Lincoln shooting. The then-popular view was that John Wilkes Booth, rather like Lee Harvey Oswald, acted alone, and we got to read about the "single-shooter theory" as mentioned in the deeply flawed Masonic cover-up known as the "Warren Commission" of 1964. I do remember noticing the remarkable coincidences of both Lincoln's and Kennedy's murders.

Here are just a few for your perusal:

1) Kennedy was elected president in 1960, Lincoln in 1860, and both men were involved in promoting black civil rights.

2) Both men were murdered on a Friday in the company of their wives.

3) Both men were mortally wounded by a bullet entering into the head.

4) Both men were succeeded by their respective vice presidents', both named Johnson, and both southerners: Andrew Johnson born in 1808, Lyndon Johnson in 1908.

5) Kennedy's secretary was a Mrs Evelyn Lincoln, and Lincoln's occasional secretary was Mary Lincoln, his wife. Both women

would grieve the loss of children; both women married in their early twenties.

There are of course many more strange similarities.

Both men's official killers (Lee Harvey Oswald and John Wilkes Booth) would themselves be murdered by a bullet. Neither would be brought to trial, and both were from the South. Both presidents were careless about their security, it seems. Both presidents had seven letters in their surnames. Although not a Freemason, Lincoln had applied for membership in 1860 but declined to be considered until after the election. He may or may not have been offered membership later in that first term of office. It seems the "Tyrian" lodge in Illinois made him an honourary member after his death, not sure why. (Reagan would also be made an honourary member later in life.) Roman Catholic John F. Kennedy, although not a Protestant Freemason, was probably a member of the Catholic Knights of St. Columba or Knights of Malta, both Catholic equivalents to the Freemasons (along with the Catenians).

During that momentous Friday morning, John Wilkes Booth had nonchalantly entered the Ford's Theatre doors. After all, he was well known at this establishment and had previously acted there before President Lincoln, then in the audience in March of 1865 appearing in the "The Apostate." That morning he had wandered in smoking his traditional cigar and would leave a half-smoked cigar in the theatre lobby when he entered that evening to murder the president in his box. However, that morning he had arrived to talk to the proprietor. Now, it seems Wilkes Booth's brother had briefly managed his theatrical career, but this time the actor was simply calling to collect his usual fan mail, a popular perk that most itinerant actors frequently took advantage of. I suppose today Wilkes Booth would be as well known to the public as say, Brad Pitt, and in his day could command a staggering salary of $20,000. So, after all, he was no stranger to the staff of this soon-to-be notorious Washington theatre. He was not himself in the play performed that evening but knew it well enough to decide the appropriate time to murder the almost defenceless president. But with Wilkes Booth, it was all in the timing, the actor's usual belief.

Later that day, Author James Swanson writes: "Booth heard the galvanizing news [that] in just eight hours the subject of all his brooding, hating and plotting would stand on the very same stone steps where he now sat reading his letter." Now, Booth would be menacingly motivated in finally dispatching this president once and for all. Previously, he had failed with others in their attempt to kidnap Lincoln, then hoping that the captured 200,000+ Confederate prisoners of war would be released in exchange for President Lincoln. Of course, it never happened due to the diligence of Alan Pinkerton, who had little faith in the usually lackadaisical Washington police force and instead used his own men to guard the president. At the time, there was no Secret Service as we know it today; later they were recruited from the Treasury in 1901 after the assassination of President McKinley, Robert Lincoln (son of Abraham Lincoln) by chance also being there.

By the way, have you ever noticed the logo that the Pinkerton national private detective agency uses? Under an all-seeing eye, it displays the words: "We never sleep." Maybe Alan Pinkerton was a Freemason himself, perhaps having been initiated in Kilwinning, the so-called famed mother lodge in Scotland where Freemasonry was supposed to have emerged, as some have seriously suggested of its birth. Later, Alan Pinkerton would suffer a serious career fallout in Washington, possibly ignited by Edwin Stanton. Pinkerton would be replaced by a Colonel Lafayette C. Baker, chief of the national detective police (NDP) and another close colleague of Edwin Stanton. This previous spymaster Baker certainly knew a lot about the Lincoln assassination and later pointed an accusing finger at Edwin Stanton as part of the plot to murder Lincoln at this time.

I'm not sure Stanton was guilty of this accusation, but he may well have had prior knowledge of a plot instigated by Booth and others to murder Lincoln. Indeed some of Stanton's later actions seem rather suspicious to me. Colonel Baker would die mysteriously, possibly by poisoning, in Washington some years later in 1868. A later medical report prepared some twenty years ago by Dr. Ray A. Neff, a professor at Indiana State University, stated that he: "performed an atomic absorption spectrophotometer analysis on strands of Lafayette Baker's hair to determine the cause of his death on July 3rd 1868. Results showed that Baker died of arsenic poisoning (possibly) from a war department employee. And we know who was the head of that important department, don't we!

Booth with this galvanising news he had just heard at the Ford Theatre would quickly assemble his willing and naïve conspirators to aid him in this Good Friday fiasco that would later witness one man dead (the president) and another missing death by a whisker's stroke (the vice president). These chosen few of Booth's band would be his willing acolytes to bring about punishment for the South's defeat and travails over those long war years under Lincoln's liberal leadership, or so Booth thought.

John Wilkes Booth, the Catholic assassin, with Masonic looking right hand

There is some doubt today if they all knew each other or had even met one another before that fateful Friday night. Some authors have suggested that Lewis Paine had not had the pleasure of meeting this ambitious actor, but there is evidence that the two had met and plotted and laughed at what they were to perform in their delusional and diabolical minds.

Let's now look at the conspirators. I have to suggest, however, that not all of them signed up to eagerly assassinate the president, and some had of course been involved in the failed previous kidnapping attempt on Lincoln. But killing a president! Well, that's another thing, they must have thought.

John Wilkes Booth, the conspiratorial black-eyed cheerleader of this motley crew, was only 26 years of age. Women adored him, men deplored him, and it is claimed he could be thoughtful and cruel, kind and conceited. Yes, he was also known as the most handsome man in America. Probably due to his professional credit, he was one of the most lucid Shakespearian actors then on the American stage, performing such memorable roles as *Othello*, *Mark Anthony*, *Hamlet*, *Richard III* and *Romeo* no less, as well as many other tragic classical roles added to this thespian's portfolio. He had even starred in a now-forgotten melodrama called *Marble Heart* with Lincoln in attendance, sitting in his box watching the performance. After Booth murdered the hapless president and wounded Major Rathbone with his sweeping knife, the assassin launched himself toward the wooden stage below (from 11 or 12 feet), and now with an injured leg, he shouted definitely to shocked spectators: "*Sic Semper Tyrannus*" or "thus always to tyrants," as remembered by Brutus in Julius Caesar.

(Latin was the governmental language pagan Rome used to kill Jesus Christ. Until recently, this same language was used by papal Rome to kill Christians and others refusing to submit to them).

I suggest this must have been his greatest and final stage performance ever to be witnessed on the open stage, and the only time he was not to be paid for his acting skills. And who knows, maybe he even had planned it that way. The conceit of the man was always alarming, it was remembered.

Previously, on April 11th, 1865, Lincoln gave a brief and unrehearsed message from the White House patio to an enthusiastic crowd and in the shadows, apparently also listening, was Wilkes Booth, who turned to a fellow conspirator standing next to him and uttered with menacing conviction: "That is the last speech he will ever give." If nothing else, Booth was always a man of his word. Later, on that infamous Good Friday, he would be the most publicly recognised assassin in history for what he did.

So, who was in the know with the actor in his previous kidnap fiasco and later involved with the murder of President Lincoln? Here are some of the main acolytes:

Lewis Powell, aged 21 and son of a Baptist minister. A look at the posed "mug" shots of the arrested conspirators taken by Alexander Gardener shows that Powell is probably the most photogenic of that prisoner portfolio. He was also one of Colonel Mosby's legendary Confederate rangers. Powell attended St. Timothy's Hall Episcopalian School along with another young co-conspirator, that being Samuel Arnold. Both met and somehow came under the persuasive personality of John Wilkes Booth, as many others had before him, it seems.

On April 14th, Lewis Powell (with the assistance of a nervous David Herold) was keeping watch outside the house of Secretary of State William H. Seward, then located on the east side of Lafayette Park (known as "the clubhouse" to Washington political insiders). In fact, Lincoln had gone to visit his injured friend, who was recovering from a road accident. Also seen at the house that evening was Edwin Stanton. Now, the conspirators' feeble plan was for Lewis Powell to enter the house, claiming to have some required medicine for Seward and stating he had come from Dr. Verdi, the family physician. Then, after gaining entry, he was to locate the Secretary of State's bedroom and kill the defenceless victim with pistol fire and, if required, to use the knife. But of course, events did not go to plan.

Secretary of State William H. Seward had previously bid for the presidency in 1860 and would the following year assist President Lincoln in preparing his inauguration speech and editing the famous Gettysburg address delivered by Lincoln in 1863. William Seward would also be prominent in the purchase of Alaska in 1867 from the bankrupt tsarist government for the princely sum of $7.2 million, eventually leading to Alaska becoming the 49th state of the Union. He also wanted to acquire Hawaii for the Union (now the 50th state) and the Virgin Islands. So, the two men were good friends and more than political rivals.

On that evening, however, the weakened William Seward was now lying on his sickbed: "His jaw broken in two places, right arm broken between shoulder and elbow, and deep bruises too numerous to count," writes James Stanton. These painful wounds were from a carriage accident he had suffered on April 5th. He had also been fitted with a heavy neck brace and this, I believe, would spare his life later that evening. By his bed sat his young daughter Fanny.

Brave young Fanny Seward with her father before the attack. Note his Masonic hand gesture!

In the unprepared house that night, Powell's terror and violence were used on two of Seward's sons, as he viciously attacked them with a knife and pistol. An injured and retired police officer was also stabbed, and a State Department messenger in the house was wounded by a stab in the back.

Four brave men would almost die in that terrible night of carnage.

Somehow, Powell reached Seward's bedroom. Now, in near darkness, Fanny raced against Powell to reach the bed, trying to throw her slender body between the huge assassin and her helpless father. What a brave girl she was! Then, young terrified Fanny would bravely grapple with Powell on the bed and be violently thrown aside, then dazed would again attempt to save her beloved father. Seward finally rolled away from the knife and out of his sickbed, but in the attempt he suffered further injuries to his face from Powell's blade, which had now slashed Seward's cheek open so viciously that the skin hung from a flap, exposing his teeth and fractured jawbone. His cheek resembled a fish gill, but he survived although his daughter feared he was dead.

Powell miserably failed in murdering his victim and then made a hasty escape before saying quietly to himself: "I'm mad, I'm mad." Seward, through unimaginable pain and the effects of shock as a wounded man, was lifted from the floor by a Sergeant Robinson and laid tenderly in his bed. He whispered: "I am not dead; send for a doctor (Verdi), send for the police, close the house."

I do wonder if he thanked the Good Lord for his escape from the jaws of death and for his precious daughter's safety; she did survive but never fully recovered emotionally. Incidentally, those blood-stained sheets can be viewed today in Seward's New York home in Auburn, and it's open to the public. William Seward afterwards would be unconscious for sixty hours, but he would live. As for young Fanny, after looking at herself in her bedroom mirror, she saw that her hands, her arms, her long and pretty dress, were all drenched in blood. She could not stop screaming. And Seward would later remark to enquiring visitors that: "His good, brave girl had done well this night." She certainly had.

Outside the Seward household, young David Herold had now beaten a hasty retreat after watching and hearing young Fanny shouting for assistance from her father's bedroom window. To me, Miss Seward is one of the heroes of this wicked failed attempt to murder a defenceless, frail, and sick man in his bed that nauseous night and nothing could have prepared her for what she suffered that night both physically and mentally. Praise also to the courage of retired Sergeant Robinson. He must also be commended, I suggest, for his bravery. And what of his later bizarre request to Edwin Stanton to keep the discarded knife that Powell had used to stab Seward and himself, Stanton granting the unusual request."

Later, a gold medal would be struck in Robinson's honour and he would also be given $5,000 in cash by Congress. On the reverse of the medal, the engraver froze Robinson and Powell in perpetual combat, the assassin raising the knife high in the air while the sergeant held the striking arm at bay." And

Steward's sons who fought so valiantly for their father's life should also be commended for their brave action in saving him. So, it seems to me God had further plans for the recovering Secretary of State and maybe his two sons.

Powell and Herold, Booth's two most loyal servants, had failed Booth in carrying out his orders. Now each man must look out for his own safety, and their futures looked grim.

Lewis Powell (the not-so-gentle giant) did not seem to have prepared a feasible escape plan for himself at all, but would later walk aimlessly in and around Washington after abandoning his horse, even attempting to sleep in trees (if this is possible) and dozing in unsecured burial vaults. He may even have tried vainly to contact the other conspirators of Booth's gang or attempted to reach an agent of Jefferson Davis without success. He then committed a huge mistake and decided to walk towards Mary Surratt's boarding house, for whatever reason, in his confused mind. He knew it well, of course, having stayed there as a boarder many times himself under different aliases, one being the popular one of being addressed as "Reverend Wood." Once there, at 11.45 pm his suspicious demeanour was noticed at the front door by one of the officers who had been dispatched to the house a second time to question Mary Surratt and other boarders at her house again. The police had previously searched for Booth and Surratt but in vain; neither were at home, it seems.

Now the lady would foolishly deny knowing who he was or why he had called at her house. Lewis had informed the questioning soldier that he had been asked to prepare a drain for her. The officer did not buy it. Then suddenly, the then-mighty Lewis Powell did something extraordinary. Inexplicably, meekly and without protest! He surrendered without a fight. After his arrest and detention, he would never walk the streets of Washington again as a free man. Unfortunately, Powell never gave a formal or public statement about those missing days before his arrest, so one can only surmise of what he hoped to achieve in his escape and where it all went wrong.

Powell and Surratt were quickly taken for questioning, with Mary Surratt begging Colonel H. H. Wells, one of Stanton's manhunters to allow her to say her prayers. She fell to her knees and prayed silently. Edwin Stanton must have been euphoric then at the fast arrest of these important conspirators, now he only needed to find the archfiend John Wilkes Booth, but that would take a little bit longer, it seems.

George Atzerodt, aged 29 and son of German immigrants, suffered from an alcohol problem, but his important use to Booth was that he was able to navigate the waters of the Potomac's dangerous swirls. He also had a knack with machinery. Booth would certainly require this man's skills in attempting to escape from the north to safety in the south. It's interesting to me that Booth didn't flee towards Canada that evening, perhaps that was a bridge too far for him to cross in seeking sanctuary whereas others did take that opportunity.

Michael O'Laughlin aged 31 was another player in this drama. His family were old friends with the Booth family in Baltimore. He was an early "suspected" conspirator and would fall under Booth's dangerous charm or charisma, it seems, and was also a member of *the Knights of the Golden Circle,* along with Booth and others. Jesse James was also a member of that notorious group of plotters, and his name would crop up years later concerning John Wilkes Booth.

Samuel Arnold, aged 31, had been at school with Booth and O'Laughlin and would be involved with the failed attempt to kidnap Lincoln as a bargaining chip for the release of Confederate prisoners of war.

David Herold, aged 21 and perhaps with learning difficulties, was employed as a chemist's shop assistant. John H. Surratt Jr., aged 20, was a former Catholic seminarian (much more on him later) along with another plotter involved in the plot, Louis J. Weichmann aged 22. Both attended the same Catholic seminary.

Weichmann's important evidence for the prosecution at the conspirators' trial would help place the waiting noose around Mary Surratt's exposed neck. This young man has been described as "a large soft youth, with a sneaking, gossipy nature wrapped up in an almost saintly manner." There has been the important unconfirmed suggestion that both Surratt and Weichmann were somehow involved in a homosexual tryst resulting in both of them leaving or being expelled from the Catholic seminary. It seems he actually shared a bedroom with John Surratt when visiting the mother's boarding house during his Washington visit.

The War Department was then under the iron control of Edwin Stanton. It has been suggested that Weichmann may have been a paid spy for Edwin Stanton and fed important information about Wilkes Booth and the suspected conspirators to Edwin Stanton or Colonel Baker. He was at Mrs Surratt's boarding house when the police originally arrived looking for Booth and John Surratt and may have tipped them off about the makeup of the house and its tenants.

Dr. Sam Mudd: now he is an interesting medic to me. He had met Booth some years before and was familiar with Booth's plans to kidnap the president and I believe he went along with it and with the future murder of Lincoln. He would later foolishly treat the wounded Booth's shattered leg in his own home. Later, under interrogation, he would deny he knew Wilkes Booth. I certainly think there is much more to learn about this mystery medic and his motives. I also do not understand why the death penalty was not used against him. Was he somehow being protected? And if so, by whom?

It seems there were others in the Lincoln plot, but all has been lost to history, with many escaping prison and the rope.

Mary E. Surratt, the so-called "mother superior" of the conspiracy: this widow, aged 44, was the landlady of a popular and, I suspect, lucrative boarding house in Washington situated on 541 H Street (and yes, it still stands today, having been converted into a Chinese or Japanese restaurant). President Andrew Johnson famously called her role in these crimes "the nest that hatched the egg" or maybe it was his spin-doctor who coined this lasting phrase.

In the coming weeks, this mother of four had a great deal of explaining to do to the police regarding her suspected aid to Booth. It's also no coincidence that four of the accused and maybe others in the plot shared the Catholic faith, with maybe even John Wilkes Booth being a recent convert, perhaps for his own personal reasons. According to some, he had in fact only converted three weeks before Lincoln's murder. However, Mrs Surratt had also been a complicit slave owner at the country tavern post office that she apparently owned and operated outside Washington City. And yes, that house is still there today, and yes, you can visit this "landmark" house.

After the Lincoln killing, Booth and Herold would together ride in haste to the tavern to collect concealed firearms and other personal effects before embarking on that southward journey they hoped would lead to freedom and perhaps fame for John Wilkes Booth.

The tavern landlord was John M. Lloyd who would later become an important prosecution witness against Mrs Surratt at the trial. I don't think there was any love lost between these two in this melodrama for whatever reason and maybe it had something to do with her religion. But, of course, plots have to be nourished and watered if they are to flower and bloom. Planning is key for any final detail to succeed, and this affair carelessly "cooked up" by Wilkes Booth within a matter of hours it would naturally lead to nothing but death for him, with death also later visiting his co-conspirators, and of course first the President of the United States. But the Holy Bible warns that: "Vengeance is mine, I will repay, saith the Lord" (Romans 12:19b).

This dire warning is something Wilkes Booth would dismiss if indeed it ever entered his conceited mind, then quickly cast it aside, rather like one of his old used theatre ticket stubs.

Fatal Shooting At The Ford

That fateful day known to this fallen world as "Good Friday" (the official day given when our Saviour died, to gloriously rise again three days later) was however traditionally a "slack day" at the theatre box office. I am sure that's not the case today.

But on this evening, excited news apparently had reached the war-weary Washingtonians that the president and perhaps General Grant would be present for that evening's sell-out performance. With over a thousand seats now occupied and perhaps standing room, the audience now waited for the president and his wife to be seated. General Lee had announced surrender, and jubilation was in the air. Nonetheless, the Lincolns were late in arriving, which must have added some sparkle to the atmosphere in the house during that historic night. Most of the paid patrons, if not all, would remember that dreadful evening for the rest of their lives rather like that Friday evening (but not Good Friday) when President Kennedy was murdered in Dallas in 1963. Do you remember it? My father did. He was seated on a 109 bus in Croydon, South London when a passenger sitting in front of him turned and asked if he had heard the shocking news.

Although unconfirmed, it seems that John Wilkes Booth had previously "checked" out the empty presidential box earlier that day and maybe drilled out a spy hole in the panel of the door to the box, and may also have had some possible assistance from Edman "Ned" Spangler, a 39-year-old Ford theatre scene shifter. He had known Booth and his family for about twelve years and had done odd jobs for them. He would later tend to Booth's waiting horse at the stage door exit, a dangerous thing to do. The police would later have him arrested for aiding the fleeing Booth because of this gesture. Booth had earlier used a prop from a wooden music stand to prop up the outer door, thereby preventing anyone on the outside from entering the box through the lobby door. Naturally, Booth did not want any complications to hinder his dramatic and theatrical escape from the theatre after the shooting. Always a "thrill seeker," perhaps he now wanted to enhance his excitement, if that's what you can call it.

Previously that evening, at 8 pm, Booth had given final orders to Lewis Powell and others perhaps by a brief note or at a group meeting to murder Secretary of State William Seward, then bed-bound as we know and recovering from a serious accident. Fellow conspirator George Atzerodt would be quickly dispatched to the Kirkwood House, where Vice President Andrew Johnson was residing, then alone and unguarded. All Atzerodt had to do was to knock on his door and, the moment Johnson opened it, plunge the knife into his chest or shoot him dead. For this, he too took a knife and a pistol, "a six-shot revolver." Of course, Arnold failed to do this, having lost his nerve: the more he drank, the worse the plan sounded, even after being fortified by large glasses of alcohol to give him "Dutch courage." He fled from the Kirkwood and was arrested some days later in his sordid hotel bedroom, and it is reported that: "He surrendered meekly not even asking why he was being taken," strange behaviour.

Edwin Stanton, the Secretary of War (Lincoln affectionately referred to him as "my Mars, god of war") would soon arrest many other suspects from the audience in the theatre that night as well as the members' cast of the play. Even the theatre owner was under suspicion. Stanton was a maniacal man with a mission who trusted no one. He believed none would escape the wrath he showed to all that happened on his watch, and he wanted blood! Of course, the starring role in this murderous melodrama would go to John Wilkes Booth. Hadn't he always yearned and craved for lasting fame? And who knows? He must have now reasoned at last that his hour had arrived at the crowded theatre.

Now joining the president and his wife that evening was Major Rathbone and his fiancée Clara Harris (more on them later). I suggest that before entering the theatre, Wilkes Booth would have fortified himself with a pre-assassination glass of whisky or a mint julep, probably prepared at "The Star," a popular tavern with the arriving and departing theatre crowd. Booth may have seen or bought a drink for the Lincolns' useless White House bodyguard, a Mr. John Parker who was noticeably absent from his post outside the presidential box that evening when the dreadful deed was committed (mighty suspicious to me by his absence). Many have suggested that Parker was implicated somehow in the plot that night, but amazingly he seems to have escaped any consequences or instant dismissal for his lack of duty that night, and in the days afterwards, he seemed to be working as usual at the White House.

He would amazingly continue his future employment in the White House guard detail until being dismissed for drunkenness. He died in 1890, and naturally Mrs Lincoln blamed him for her husband's murder. She didn't think much of Andrew Johnson, her husband's successor either, and would later call the Ford's Theatre "that dreadful house, that dreadful house." A very perceptive lady it seems.

Once Booth entered the hushed theatre without being observed (or so he thought), he then proceeded through the hall towards the presidential box, which he found to be unguarded, with Lincoln's servant Charles Forbes seated nearby. Booth nodded to him and then showed him a visiting card that seemed to satisfy the servant's curiosity; maybe he was a fan of Booth, like many others. Booth must also have known that Lincoln's bodyguard Parker was not at his post, maybe having left him in the tavern next door slurping his beer.

This now leaves the coast clear for Booth to silently enter the box (there could have been some new thick-pile carpet fitted in the box that day that would have certainly deadened any sound). Inside, Lincoln was sitting comfortably in a rocking chair. Booth now observed him through a prepared peephole that he or someone has cut out that day. Then at 10:13 pm, he now silently entered the box and waited for the punch line from the play he had himself seen many times but apparently never acted in it. This punchline was delivered by an actor from the stage and normally brought an avalanche of laughter, thus simply drowning out the single shot fired by Booth.

Yes, he seemed to have thought of everything, hadn't he? Now armed with a small Derringer .44 calibre pistol that almost fit his right hand and with a vicious Rio Grande camp knife clutched in the other, Booth prepared to place pressure on the trigger and stand dangerously close behind the unsuspecting Abraham Lincoln, then paused. History was about to be executed in more ways than one on that fatal Friday evening at the Ford.

Original playbill with bloodstained at the bottom

As the expected laughter exploded through the blue smoke of cigarettes and cigars and from the fog of the auditorium gas lights, Booth raised his gun and aimed at Lincoln's unexposed head, then fired the projectile, which swiftly entered beneath Lincoln's left ear, passing through the lateral sinus and then coming to rest behind his right eye. Lincoln silently slumped forward as if asleep, it seems. Major Rathbone, as a military man, recognised the sound of a gunshot and saw an intruder in the box and leapt to his feet to face the armed assailant, who shouted: "Freedom!" The two met, then grappled, with Rathbone being badly injured between the elbow and shoulder by the raised knife, with his own blood spurting out like a tap. Booth then prepared to jump some 12 feet from the box, a foolish thing to do, I suggest, but in his haste to escape Rathbone's outstretched hands, his boot spur caught in a flag or bunting, causing him to land awkwardly on the stage, fracturing his left tibia several inches above the ankle, unbeknownst to him. Turning towards a stunned audience, with many thinking this was part of the play, Booth brandished the blood-stained knife on high, shouting those stirring words: "*Sic Semper Tyrannus*" or "Thus always to tyrants," the proud state motto of Virginia and the motto of the famous 149th American fighter squadron.

Further adding to those stirring words, Booth then proclaimed: "The South is avenged." Or so he hoped. But there was no applause, only shocked silence. Hadn't he always adored the copious applause offered to him after so many previous performances in so many theatres, but tonight his audience was pained and perplexed. "What is going on?" they enquired of each other. Booth did not pause, but rushed towards the waiting exit where he was heard to say (to no one in particular): "I have done it."

Some authors have suspected that he shouted those Latin words from the box before he made his momentous jump downwards. But I do not think he would have had time to deliver his speech and fight off Rathbone's furious attack as well. Perhaps he had it in mind to first address the audience seated below him with flowery eloquence from the presidential box, but it was not to be.

Timing is the basic requirement of any actor's stage training, and Booth did what he could amongst all the confusion in the Ford Theatre that night. He departed and without an encore, it seems. Interestingly, Colonel Baker's police later searched and ransacked Edman Spangler's house for evidence tying him to the plot, discovering a heavy knotted rope. Was this, they suggested, perhaps to be used by the fleeing Booth to descend or swing from the box instead of jumping onto the wooden stage? Who knows!?!

At last, he must think of his safety in the so-called "Baptist Alley," thus named because the theatre had previously been an abode of worship. He breathlessly and painfully hobbled out of that theatre turmoil, slowly mounted his waiting bay mare we are informed perhaps by Spangler, marked with a white star on her forehead, soon to gallop feverishly into the pages of history. Sadly, the horse was later destroyed by fellow conspirator and riding companion David Herold. Soon, the fleeing pair crossed separately over heavily guarded Washington Navy Bridge that night. For now, I find this to be a mystery, to be examined in a later chapter.

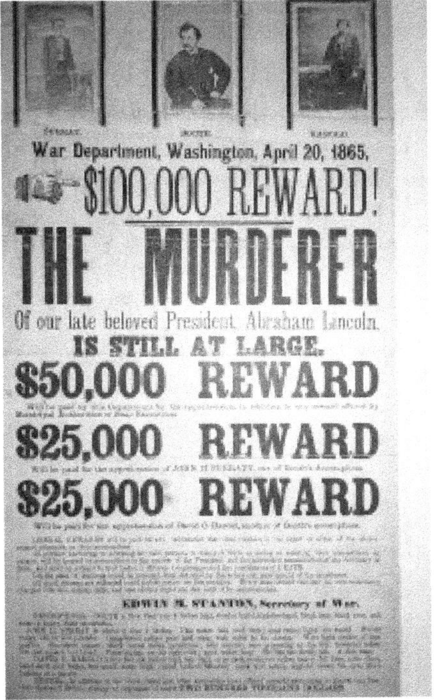

Original reward poster with Herold's name spelt wrong

This was the final stage performance that John Wilkes Booth would ever perform alive again on any American stage. To the south, he would become a legend and a hero (and maybe still is!) and to the north, he was simply a liar and murderer and a "disgrace to the acting profession," according to one actor/manager.

Most importantly, the 16th president of the Union was now fatally wounded and lying comatose in his chair.

Pandemonium was now witnessed in the Ford's Theatre, as the stunned and bewildered audience tried to grasp what had happened in their midst on that awful Good Friday evening of 1865, a year burned forever into the pages of history.

Seen earlier, loitering outside the front of the theatre, was a very important conspirator, namely, John Harrison Surratt, previously a Confederate courier and maybe Wilkes Booth's number one assistant in the plot. This young man's misplaced loyalties were certainly with the embattled South and always had been. That evening, the wily nervous 21-year-old (or someone fitting his description) was observed to be coordinating events outside the theatre by excited theatre-goers, and holding a pocket watch or stopwatch. He may even have been clutching an ebony rosary in one hand, as he was very religious after all (we always say get out of organised religion now and into a lasting relationship with Jesus Christ).

Perhaps the successful shooting of the president was somehow coordinated with the terrible attack at William Seward's home by Lewis Powell. I suggest that as the distraught crowds later poured out of the grieving theatre, Surratt heard of what had occurred inside the building. Then, with hundreds of others, he waited and witnessed the dying president being carried by Dr. Leale and others out of the boarding house opposite the theatre. It must have dawned on Surratt what Booth had done and to an innocent man, and more importantly, that he was involved. Then, quickly in the next few hours, he would flee the locked-down city in panic, now aided by Catholic priests and maybe by a Jesuit to numerous parish safe houses, heading towards Canada. Later he would leave by ship under an assumed alias of John Watson (very original) and be taken to Europe, there to eventually arrive in Italy at the welcoming gates of the Vatican.

Once there, he would enlist with the "Papal Zouaves," that colourful silly uniformed army of the Papal States. "Surratt blended in with the Catholic milieu, and he felt safely beyond the reach of the manhunters." But this would all change dramatically for him the following year and end in an amazing court case brought against him by the U.S. government, leading to an even bizarre ending.

After Booth's defiant deed, it would take an exhaustive 12-day manhunt initiated on the personal orders of Secretary of War Edwin M. Stanton, some claiming that he has been America's only dictator and the man who apparently kept his deceased wife in his bedroom in her coffin and conversed with her daily, and a deceased daughter in her bedroom using the same procedure. I do wonder what the servants in the Stanton house made of all this, if indeed true.

Now with over 2,000 serving soldiers at Edwin Stanton's disposal and a generous reward offer thrown into this American tragedy, Stanton soldiers would search and secure John Wilkes Booth if possible, and until that day or hour would hunt him down like a rabid dog. Of course, this was never what the delusional John Wilkes Booth had ever wished for or wanted for his "rightful" place in history. Hadn't he always demanded better things for his family and himself? But this was just the beginning of a mystery that perhaps ended with his death in 1865, or perhaps not. Maybe the story of John Wilkes Booth would offer another ending in 1903.

Rare and unused 1965 stamp

Chapter 2: "High Drama At The Ford Theatre"

———

As the wounded and now-expiring president lay awkwardly on the carpet of the crowded box, there was an air of pain and panic from those standing helplessly around him, most of them uncertain and unprepared as to what was happening. However, outside the theatre John Wilkes Booth was now preparing his hurried "flight plan" for escape, to be joined later by the gullible and frightened co-conspirator, David "Davy" Herold.

It seems these fleeing fugitives had arranged an appointment at the dubious Surratt Tavern and previously: "Booth has instructed Mary to tell the tavern keeper John Lloyd, a heavy drinking and former Washington policeman to whom she had rented her country place, to get everything ready for the actor's visit this evening." Once there, the two would collect rifles and an important spyglass; it might be good news as far as they are concerned, but John Lloyd's later litany of lies spewed out on a hot June day at the trial concerning what Booth and Herold had collected and concealed that fateful night would assist the prosecution to secure the hangman's rope around the necks of four of the seated conspirators.

Earlier on that fateful Good Friday, after failing in his amateur attempt to assassinate Secretary of State Seward, Lewis Powell fled the scene of his crime like a scared rabbit and went into hiding. He would later arrive suspiciously on the doorstep of Mrs Mary Surrat's boarding house at 10:30 pm with a suspicious shovel or pick axe held on his shoulder. Unfortunately for him, armed soldiers had arrived earlier and were searching this infamous boarding house, having been informed of the possible Booth/John Surratt connection, and Lewis Powell's suspicious movements alerted them when he knocked on the door. After this, he would never go back to wandering the leafy streets of Washington as a freeman ever again.

The 21-year-old Lewis Powell/Payne would somehow later claim that Mrs Mary Surratt had asked him previously to prepare a ditch, yet when confronted with this information in the hall by the captain of the guard, she would vehemently deny it saying: "Before God, I do not know this man and have never seen him before. I did not hire him to dig a gutter for me." He had in fact stayed frequently at her boarding house, posing convincingly as Reverend Wood; his father was a minister, it seems. Lewis Powell may well have previously been a spy operating for the Confederate Secret Service, it has been suggested, or maybe he was just a failed actor who liked dressing up. A big mistake, I suggest, by Mary Surratt being caught out in her lies. The Surratt boarding house must also have captured the imagination of most of her neighbours because there was jubilation throughout the city when General Lee surrendered his troops. Her house, however, apparently failed to display any festive Union flags. Also, the following day, when the death of the president was announced, her house displayed none of the traditional black bunting or black drapes usually seen adorning windows and doors as a mark of mourning and respect. This would certainly have made the police suspicious of where the Surratt household's true loyalties indeed lay, or maybe she was just an attention seeker or whatever expression they used in those days. It would only have been a matter of days before "the law" came calling on the lady of the house again, only this time they would not leave empty-handed, as they had previously.

Drama at the Ford Theatre

At the theatre during the crowded pandemonium, Miss Laura Keene - the popular star of the play - had elbowed her way somehow up into the crowded box after witnessing and hearing the commotion in and around its limited space. Now lying before her was the president whom she may have met previously; he lay mortally wounded on the floor but was still breathing. To her, he would always be her president, but now he looked defenceless and alone: "The scene riveted Keene and excited her theatrical instincts." Yet she was confused and concerned for his creature comfort and would enquire in a whisper if she could perhaps cradle his bleeding head in her lap if possible. Dr Charles Leale, the young 23-year-old U.S. assistant surgeon in attendance volunteered; he had only qualified some six weeks earlier. In uniform, he slowly turned towards a sobbing Mary Todd Lincoln, somehow silently requesting her agreement. Mrs Lincoln gave her consent, then turned towards Dr Leale to ask in a pleading voice: "Oh physician, is he dead? Can he recover?" He could only ponder her sadness before turning back to his patient. As regards Miss Keene's many motives and of what she achieved that evening it has been written that: "She knew that history was being made in that box, and she had convinced herself that she must be a part of it." Her place in history is now secure and it "closed the curtain on Laura Keene's maudlin, private drama. Her fame guaranteed," so writes author James Swanson.

Later she was seen in "disarray, hair dishevelled, not only was her gown soaked in Lincoln's blood but her hands and even her cheeks where her fingers had strayed were bedaubed with the sorry stains. The actress who began the night in a light comic role now looked like an apparition from a nightmare." There is some serious doubt that maybe those blood splatters on her dress were perhaps not only Lincoln's blood because he had apparently bled very little from the head wound and perhaps most of it had emerged from the seriously wounded Major Rathbone who was still bleeding profusely from a deep arm "slash" delivered by a demented Booth. Clara Harris, the wounded major's fiancée "who had seen the whole thing, never forgot the forceful swing of Booth's practised and powerful arm." Rathbone would naturally have been hovering close to the fallen president with so much of his own blood accidentally dripping onto Keene's silk dress. This is an important possibility to consider and I think the suggestion does make sense.

Major Rathbone

Laura Keene's dress was spared the drenching that saturated the garments of Fanny Seward and Clara Harris (Rathbone's fiancée). Fanny and Clara's dresses did not survive. But Laura Keene cherished the blood – and brain – speckled frock from that terrible night, according to James Swanson. In fact, she would later be detained with the confused cast of the play for questioning by the police, and it seems many from the audience as well! What a night it must have been for all concerned!

It was then decided, perhaps by collective decision, to journey with the president away from the frenetic atmosphere of the theatre, but surprisingly not to the empty White House as would have been expected. This latter option was apparently discounted due to the distance and the decrepit state of the roads. Instead, the unprepared Dr Leale had decided that a nearby boarding house would have to do. This spot was popularly known as the William Person boarding house, a three-story brick-constructed house, and was convenient for the caravan of medics to reach. Situated opposite the Ford Theatre it would now have to act as a makeshift basic field hospital to care for America's dying commander-in-chief now arriving at the front door cautiously opened by one of the boarders, a Mr Henry Safford. The president was carried by the struggling bearers up the curved eight steps and was now seen in a collapsed, almost sitting position, yet his head hung listless down on his chest, and he looked dreadful. Lincoln was then taken to an unoccupied bedroom. It seems the room's tenant was out celebrating the end of the War (but not Mrs Surratt! More on him later), and won't this man have a surprise when he returns to his room from the city's festivities of fireworks and fun!

Dr. Charles Leale in old age

For some reason, this favoured room had apparently been previously occupied only the year before when John Wilkes Booth was himself performing at the Ford Theatre. Not only had he booked in at the same boarding house, but he amazingly occupied the same bedroom where the president now hovered between life and death. What a bizarre coincidence! Now inside the crowded room, Lincoln was laid diagonally on the bed due to his height (6' 4"), and the long and lonely vigil began for those seated or standing around the borrowed bed (with many coming and going, it seems) as the president silently hovered between life and death.

Later he would be stripped of his clothes and tenderly wrapped in heavy army blankets with heated china hot-water bottles to conserve his body heat, and with additional bottles of brandy used to hopefully revive both Lincoln and some of the shocked onlookers. Also brought into the equation was a mustard plaster bath fitted around the president's dying body. Outside the theatre, a crescendo of shouting was heard in the air as people grappled with the terrible news that: "They have shot the president...." "Kill the rebels"... "Kill the traitors" or "Oh no, it can't be true." Also heard as a lament would be: "Who did it and why?" These were just some of the confused and blaspheming voices lamenting that night's events.

It seems the jubilation of the earlier surrender has turned into tears of shame, shock and sadness. Washington has never witnessed anything like this high drama being played out before them. Heard in the confusion of the boarding house was Mrs Mary Lincoln screaming: "They've killed him, they've killed him." No one is sure who she was referring to or why. The grieving Mrs Lincoln had been followed into the sweltering room by a wounded Major Rathbone, his army uniform sleeve now soaked in blood, along with his shocked fiancé Miss Harris, and Miss Laura Keene bringing up the rear (yes, her again). Then "doctor Leale leaned in close to the president's face and nods, he was still alive." Mary Lincoln now agreed to depart the small sleeping room, but she would return later. Her eldest son Captain Robert Lincoln also arrived with Miss Clara Harris and Laura Keene (yes, her), all to wait and maybe pray with all eyes on Mrs Mary Lincoln staring into a coal grate. All silently prepared themselves for the doctor's unrehearsed prognosis on the fallen president's deteriorating condition, and most now painfully aware that it doesn't look promising.

Later that evening, against the wishes of his friends, Vice President Johnson would arrive and go to Lincoln's bedside and gaze soberly at the dying Lincoln. He departed soon after but before that, he would say a few silent words to Mrs Lincoln before wandering off into the night, probably never to see Lincoln alive again: "He will choose not to assert himself, instead he will leave it to Edwin Stanton to search for Lincoln's murderers and bring them to a swift slice of justice.

"The doctors meanwhile probed the wound of the president with their bare, unsanitary fingers, sticking their pinkies inside Lincoln's brain because there was work to do inside Lincoln's brain." Poor man and he's not even dead yet! This crude procedure reads like a pre-autopsy examination, does it not? Meanwhile, 13 miles outside the city, John Wilkes Booths and fellow co-conspirator David Herold have now the empty dark road to themselves and both confident they would escape the pursuing police as they make for that drinking tavern owned by Mrs Mary Surratt in Surrattsville to collect those importantly needed firearms and a spyglass.

Booth's escape incensed, but thrilled the nation. Photographs of him became so popular that the government soon banned their sales, and "fantasy prints showed Satan whispering in Booth's ear moments before he shot Lincoln." Seems they couldn't get enough of Johnny Wilkes Booth, and wouldn't he have loved such notoriety!?

Throughout the night a procession of the high and mighty of Washington's political and possibly Masonic circles arrived to look at the unconscious Lincoln. Edwin Steer, the author of *Blood on the Moon*, estimates over 58 people were wandering in and out of the stifling bedroom that night with additional household servants and others being "press-ganged" into carrying and emptying overflowing chamber pots throughout the night. I suppose someone had to do it and of course, with no indoor plumbing then operating in the house I can understand why. Oh, and thank goodness Dr Samuel Mudd wasn't one of the attending doctors standing around Lincoln's bedstead that night! But more on him later.

One important man who would arrive soon after the shooting and naturally place armed soldiers at the front door of the house and elsewhere throughout the city now on lockdown would be the Secretary of War, Edwin McMasters Stanton. In the next few frantic days in American history, this gentleman would become the most powerful "unelected" man in Washington, if not America, pulling all government strings towards himself without interference, it seems, from anyone. But what motivated him in what he attempted to achieve that night? Was it ambition or guilt, or perhaps both? It seems Stanton was a complex man in his private and public life. After his arrival: "The Peterson boarding house was (to become) the War Department tonight."

After visiting the dying president's bedroom, he would be informed by Dr. Leale: "It is hopeless. Mr. Stanton quickly commandeers the Peterson back parlour as the temporary seat of government. There he can also observe any coming and goings from the front entrance."

If Lincoln's failing body was in the fragile hands of the attending doctors, then America was in the capable hands of Edwin Stanton, with all power now being invested by himself into his hands. This lawyer's grip was secure. Stanton would not cease, it seems, until the capture and punishment of Wilkes Booth and his co-conspirators, and that included Mrs Mary Surratt. "Hundreds of telegrams were dispatched by Stanton and his minions that night. Soon the wire sang back with messages to Stanton from military commanders. We have received your news. We are obeying your orders."

All Union soldiers quickly marched to the beat of Edwin "Mars" Stanton's tempo. This man was to be obeyed, and without question, it seems! This to me is awesome, ambitious and naked power that perhaps even Abraham Lincoln never possessed or wanted for his own use from the Oval Office in the White House.

Whilst Secretary of War, Stanton had never had a lot of time for Lincoln, it seems. Their social backgrounds were so different. Hadn't he called Lincoln "weak kneed" and been often patronising to the president, although I'm not sure Lincoln even noticed or cared about Stanton's sharp sarcastic tongue. However, that night when Stanton entered the boarding house we are informed that: "His nerves were jumping like devils. Always erratic, Stanton was now in a panic his energy sometimes brilliant sometimes rash. He believed himself to be the real ruler of the nation with his superior brain unlike the softer will of Lincoln. Yet ferocious headaches had racked the Secretary for years, asthma tore at his throat and a phobia which unbalanced his brain whenever he was near a corpse." I can see how the corpse phobia would affect some people.

Now at 56 years old, destiny had led him to this house and his role in history was being played out all around him without a script or a director. He gazed down at the wounded Lincoln. Then turning and hearing Mrs Lincoln's sobbing he ordered an aide to: "Get that woman out of here." He was instantly obeyed and she, poor lady, would be taken and settled into a small cluttered parlour." "Stanton was now Czar." This man would not abdicate one iota of his naked power and privilege nor would he allow it to be taken from him. Destiny (he may convince himself) or God, for that matter, had designed him for this supporting role and he would disappoint no friend or fool in twisting its talents. Nor would he allow anyone to obstruct him or divert him in playing out the final scenes in this American tragedy. Edwin McMasters Stanton was a man with a mission, and "Mars" was in a hurry, it seems.

Stanton somehow, it seems to me, was rather slow off the mark in issuing orders in apprehending the suspect Wilkes Booth. After all, he had been identified after the shooting by most of the theatre staff and some of the audience. So, what was the delay? Stanton, I suggest, had also been made aware early that evening (perhaps by Col. Lafayette Baker, head of the self-styled national detective police, or one of his favourites) of potentially important street information from the colonel's army of paid "informers" that named Wilkes Booth as the prime suspect, and it seems he had a suspicious connection somehow to a southern sympathiser, a certain John Harrison Surratt, the late postmaster of the tavern in Surratsville.

With this crucial information gained from who else but the military police, they would pay a surprise visit on April 14th to that "widow woman's" boarding house, Mary Surratt's establishment, and would inquire into the whereabouts of her son John. She would be unable to assist with their enquires as her son John was away, it seems, somewhere on business, possibly in Canada, or on "rebel business" perhaps.

Surprisingly, they departed, much to her relief, only to return later. It is odd to me that only hours after the Ford Theatre shooting, with the police politely knocking at Mrs Surratt's front door, that they then departed quickly after a cursory search of the premises.

So, were they warned away and if so, by whom? Three days later on April 17th, they returned, now under the command of a suspicious Major W.H. Smith whose orders were clear and to the point: Arrest the residents and search the premises! Some new important information may be received by Lafayette Baker and with Stanton's knowledge, led them to this house of treason. It did not look good for the Surratt house on 541, also known as 604 H Street, this being the house of many crimes and secrets, and all would be revealed.

Years later Major Smith would recall: "It was odd. Mrs Surratt did not ask even for what she was arrested for, and expressed no surprise or feeling at all." All very strange in this Washington melodrama. As written earlier, the stupid co-conspirator Lewis Powell made an unexpected entry at the boarding house and would be taken away with the other tenants for further questioning. Included in this dragnet was an innocent Anna Surratt and other boarders, including an 11 year old schoolgirl who lived alone without her parents at Mary Surratt's. I wonder what this little girl's sad story was.

Mrs Surratt would be immediately transported to the old capitol prison. Not so many others caught up in this drama! They would be held in cramped and stinking ship holds, these being the "Montauk and the Saugus." Some earlier suspects would be released before the trial of the eight began, and these were the fortunate ones.

Later, the soldiers would search the boarding house and unearth "incriminating evidence," it seems, including small arms ammunition, a photo of President Jefferson Davis and the coup de grâce: a picture of John Wilkes Booth hidden behind the picture frame. This would certainly go against Mrs Surratt and the other seven co-conspirators who would make their public appearances later in shackles before the nine seated military prosecution officers of the Union Army.

Interestingly, some years later General Thomas Maley Harris, one of the commission judges, wrote a book detailing his research that the church of Rome was implicated in the president's murder, and he always remained emphatic in this belief. And from what I have discovered so far, it seems the general was correct in his research about the wicked Catholic church!

Just a small insight that should be mentioned, I think, concerning the arrest of Lewis Powell, a.k.a. Payne: if he had not arrived unexpectedly on the doorstep of the Surratt boarding house that fatal night "he might have escaped Washington and vanished from history," speculates James Swanson and I think he is correct in this view. And as for Powell's insanity plea that was raised at the trial by his defence, it seems he suffered serious constipation cramps and just needed a simple laxative. Of course it didn't help his defence when Secretary of State William Seward's wife Frances Adeline died just two months after the attempted murder of her husband during the trial, either from a heart attack or perhaps from the shock of what she had seen brutally inflicted on her family when Lewis Powell crossed her family threshold with murder in his heart, only to fail miserably. All at a terrible price, it seems, for her and her young daughter and her sons as well.

Authors David Balsiger and Charles E. Selier Jr. claim: "Payne and Powell were separate individuals. The authors have obtained civil war service records on both individuals as well as confession statements by conspirators, Michael Olaughlin and George Atzerodt, stating that Payne and Powell were separate individuals here. The authors believe the new evidence indicates that Payne was arrested and framed for his cousin's evil deeds." Yet confusingly we are informed that: "within hours of Powell's arrest William Bell, William Seward's servant, had clearly identified Powell as the knife-wielding maniac." There might be some truth in this presented information, but then is it not all part of the Lincoln conspiracy that has left so many unanswered questions that may never be convincingly answered and perhaps never will be.

Meanwhile, Edwin Stanton issued countless crucial orders as secretary for war in the Lincoln cabinet, but this night in the Peterson house, one crucial order he would dispatch was for all Washington bridges to be sealed to prevent Booth from escaping, or maybe also to prevent still active Confederate spies from entering the darkened city, as the country lay still witnessing the pangs of a weary war with suspected agent provocateurs plotting among the community.

Amazingly, however, escapee John Wilkes Booth did seemingly crossing the Navy Yard Bridge by offering a bizarre password to an enquiring sentry, a certain Sergeant Silas Cobb, then on duty. That mysterious word was "TBR" and amazingly, as they fell from his parched lips, he was allowed to cross unchallenged. Later, David Herold would also find it simple to gallop over the same bridge. Another mystery rider that night and now entering this plot was a certain Edwin Henson, a suspected drug smuggler and friend of Wilkes Booth who also seems to have been able to ride across that same guarded bridge. It's all amazing to me the amount of unchallenged outward traffic that night departing from a so-called locked down and secured Washington.

As regards the mysterious "TBR" uttered by Wilkes Booth. I can only speculate it means perhaps "Tobacco Road" where later coincidently, it seems, Wilkes Booth or someone else posing as him would be surrounded by soldiers in a large tobacco-curing shed, of all places. There he would be cornered to be smoked out and wounded at Garrett's farm. But whom, I wonder, provided Booth with that "magical" escape password that led to his temporary freedom that night? Perhaps someone associated with the entourage of Andrew Johnson, the Vice President.

Another unexplained mystery from that night's "comings and goings" that has never been satisfactorily explained is who "for hours after the murder blacked out commercial telegraph lines from Washington," and on whose orders? Yet the local inhabitants of a hamlet in outer Washington had heard somehow that very afternoon of the shooting of the president, all very strange and rather similar to what happened hours before the Kennedy shooting in Dallas in 1963 when some headlines around the world proclaimed "Kennedy Dead." All very bizarre in both cases.

Earlier that fateful Friday morning, John Wilkes Booth learned the staggering news relayed to him by an excited Henry Clay Ford that the president and his guests, with perhaps general Grant, would be attending his theatre that very evening to watch Laura Keene appear in the thousandth performance of *Our American Cousin*. Hearing this, Booth must have almost danced an Irish jig in excitement at what he had just learned about the man he had loathed for so long, the man he blamed for what this cruel Civil War had inflicted on his beloved "Gallant South" under Lincoln's command.

After gathering some of his coterie of co-conspirators for briefings that evening he later decided to compose some final letters. Always cautious in promoting his conceited image, in room 228 at the National Hotel he now committed to paper some of his reasons for what was about happen to Lincoln. Once he had completed his task, he would sign his own name as well as add, perhaps as an afterthought, the names of Lewis Powell/Paine, David Herold and George Atzerodt.

Later, at 11:30 pm he would pay a visit to Mrs Surrat's boarding house, probably to prepare and finalise his escape plans from the city, there with Mrs Surratt and maybe her son listening in rapt attention about what he wished to achieve for the south and himself of course. Unbeknownst to them both and silently watching was Lewis Weichmann, one of John Surratt's old school buddy "who remembered that he witnessed his landlady and Booth in earnest discussion." Later, back on the street, Booth encountered a fellow actor, a Mr John Matthews. The two men were apparently old friends, with Matthews coincidently appearing that evening at the Ford Theatre in *Our American Cousin*, can you believe? Booth then sought a favour of this old friend and offered him a sealed letter requesting that it be sent to the *National Intelligencer*, a daily newspaper (now defunct), for the following day's publication and for the attention of the editor James C. Welling, probably to be delivered by hand. "Matthews accepted the sealed envelope and slipped it into a coat pocket."

That letter will be inserted in full later in this book. A second Booth letter seems to have arrived on the editor's desk (not sure how). "The letter rambles on, disjointed, the product of an aggravated and anguished mind." The letter attacks and names thirty-five speculators and politicians who, Booth claims, will exploit the now bloody and defeated southern states. The letter was never published.

Another letter will reach Vice President Johnson's secretary Col. Browning, but was Browning really Booth's friend (it has been asked), because now Booth blames Browning for not seeing him when he called at the "Kirkwood house" earlier. It seems he would quote poetry, maybe some Shakespeare, in his letter to the colonel. But the point of it all remains unknown unless, of course, both Browning and Johnson were personally involved in this presidential plot to assassinate President Lincoln. Perhaps this letter was written in some form of code known only to Booth and Browning. Didn't Booth always love the dramatic? You also have to ask yourself, of course, who benefited most by removing a sitting president, and of course, it's the immediate vice president, who would naturally occupy the departed king's throne. But perhaps uneasy lay his own crown as well (in 1868, some years later, Johnson would be impeached). Politics, as they say, is a dirty business.

In their 1977 book *The Lincoln Conspiracy*, authors Balsiger and Sellier write that Lafayette Baker had written an undated letter to Secretary of War Stanton. It reads: "It is essential that I see you at once in regards to the card of Booth's left for Andrew Johnson. I have most confidential information to relate concerning Booth's acquaintance with president Johnson and others which you will find alarming. Your obedient servant Lafayette C. Baker." I think this crucial letter proves that Booth was connected with Andrew Johnson and perhaps other cabinet members in murdering the defenceless President Lincoln at the Ford Theatre that night. However, I do not believe William Seward was in on this plot, although he may well have heard rumours about it. Did Edwin Stanton ever learn more about this "alarming" news from Baker? And if he did, would he have acted upon this "crucial" information or just sat on it? Well, who knows? I think by then, the die in the conspiracy had been cast and the future litany of lies that would be spewed out during the coming military trial was being written by complicit men and rehearsed to be recited later to perfection by them and their cohorts.

It gets interesting because it seems that later that night, after Booth's friend and fellow actor John Matthews had witnessed the commotion that had gone from shock to sadness outside the Ford Theatre after the shooting of Lincoln, he may possibly have actually witnessed the dying president in transit from the theatre to the boarding house, but was unaware of who the escaping assailant was. Later, the poor man would nearly be lynched by an angry mob mistaking him for John Wilkes Booth and it seems there was indeed a similarity in appearance between the two men and maybe Matthews acted as an understudy for Booth in previous plays. More important is that even the baying crowd knew whom or had learned in some way or another that Wilkes Booth was the suspected shooter in the Ford Theatre and was responsible for the president's wounds. Now with the fear of what he had heard about Booth and that he might be a prime suspect in the Booth connection he quickly returned to his rented room and opened the letter to read its contents, probably several times. Then he decided to destroy its contents by quickly tossing the letter into the fireplace where it would burn to ashes.

Fortunately, Matthews possessed an eidetic memory. After all, he is a trained Shakespearean actor and years later would be able to recite it to an enquiring journalist. Amazingly, it seems, his rented room was situated in the Peterson boarding house, of all places. In other words, as he destroyed Booth's incriminating letter by consigning it to the flames of history, the dying President Lincoln was fading away fast just a few floors below Matthews' room. If correct, this is amazing and I still find it difficult to believe these events took place. But the truth, they say, is stranger than fiction.

Now returning to the dramatic events after the shooting: an unprepared Dr Charles Leale would be a prominent player in one of the most iconic scenes portrayed in American history, maybe even more so than the gunning down of John F Kennedy in Dallas, and that's saying something.

Six confused and shocked perspiring men, two of them being Dr Taft and Dr King, carried the tall fallen president, their own commander-in-chief, with Dr Teal leading the way, supporting the president's dropping head. They finally departed the mayhem of the Ford Theatre and moved into the gathering crowd outside. There, the dancing gaslights cast a ghostly and unreal Luminas light on the now-paused presidential party which looked as if they were attending a wake, and in a strange sort of way they were, except the body they guarded wasn't cold as yet. Surrounding them now was a gathering of onlookers of nearly one thousand Washingtonians, whose fallen faces showed a shocking picture of sadness and traces of fear diluted with grief etched on so many enquiring faces. Some were praying silently, their dry lips moving in an unheard whisper.

Many would lean forward and touch this wounded president as he was carried past them rather like touching a dead "saint's" relic.

On Tenth Street outside the boarding house, I suspect it was probably unpaved with the then daily debris of a city being revelled and covering almost every inch including freshly dropped horse manure that had yet to be cleared away by refuse collectors, if at all. Dr Leale now slowly paused in the middle of the road and realised the agitated president was straining for air. He paused where he stood and still desperately searched for a safe house, his eyes alighting on a possible refuge. After furtive knocking on the oak door by a soldier, no one answered, at least not yet. No one was at home or wished to open that saving door. Dr Leale then acted quickly concerning the president's laboured breathing and using his finger, he "yanks a blood clot from the hole in Lincoln's head to relieve the pressure on the brain and tosses the gooey mass into the street. Fresh blood and brain matter oozed through Dr. Leale's fingers." Minutes later, this human caravan of death was slowly admitted into the Peterson boarding house then owned by William A. Peterson, a bespoke German tailor by trade.

The front door was slowly opened by one of the shocked tenants, who slowly admitted the uninvited guests. History would be acted out in this unlikely unassuming house in the long night ahead. But now the dying president was carried carefully up the eight steps, almost in a sitting position, it seems, to the open and now-welcoming front door. Some of the crowds stood outside silently watching and weeping and unknown to them: "This would be the last time Americans saw Abraham Lincoln alive," writes James Swanson, and sadly Lincoln will never leave the house alive either.

Later, in the now silent boarding house, it had been a long exhausting night and at 7:20 am the following morning the 56 year old Abraham Lincoln's pulse began to deteriorate. There were possibly 22 people now standing silent and alert in that claustrophobic room, only able to watch and wait for the welcome end of their own discomfort and listen to the president's agony as he gasped his last breath.

Mrs Lincoln was noticeably absent but Edwin "Mars" Stanton was not. He now stood erect like a silent sentinel at the bedside watching his president's life slowly ebb away like a retreating tide deserting the shore. But just somehow, I suggest, he was a changed man after all of this, because he was now no longer Lincoln's foe but a friend, albeit it a late one. From now on, he would do all he could to secure Lincoln's place in history, commencing of course with the coming funeral arrangements to be tailor-made for a president in a manner fitting even for a king. It would be a display of grief previously unseen in this young republic yet to gain its supremacy.

At 7:20 am, exhausted and emotional Dr Charles, who had been at Lincoln's side for 9 hours, placed his hand on the president's right radial pulse. At 7:22 and 55 seconds, it was over. He was gone. "He is dead," one of the doctors said. I suggest it was Dr Leale whose unexpected tenure as the president's attending physician was now finally complete and his place in history now as secure as the Rock of Gibraltar.

There was silence for a few minutes, Lincoln's pastor then summoned from the church (he very rarely attended) to recite a useless prayer over the corpse and "that later not even he could remember what he had said," the pastor would sadly recall to friends who enquired of what he had uttered that morning.

It fell to Edwin Stanton to shatter the overwhelming silence by declaring: "Now he belongs to the angels." Others claim that he whispered: "Now he belongs to the ages" to no one in particular. This sounds to me more like Edwin Stanton's vocabulary.

The exhausted Dr Leale closed the dead man's eyes, placing coins on each of the eyes and then drew up the sheet. It is reported he had held the dying president's hand all night, a labour of love he would later remember when asked to recall that night at the Peterson boarding house.

One man at the Ford Theatre that night and apparently later present at the Peterson boarding house as well as Horatio O. Cooke, one of Lincoln's successful spies and friends. After the War had ended in 1865, he became a professional magician and "near the end of his life, he became close friends with Houdini."

Later, sitting alone in the bedroom with Lincoln, Edwin Stanton retrieved a small pair of silver scissors from his jacket pocket and cut a generous lock of hair, more than a hundred strands and sealed it in a small envelope for Mrs Mary Wells, the wife of the Secretary of the Navy and a friend of Mrs

Lincoln. A nice but rather macabre gesture from a man who did not care to be around corpses, it seems.

The only evidence of how that bedroom appeared soon after the president had been taken away is seen in a grainy picture of the bedroom taken by one of the two enterprising boarders then living in the house, they being Henry and Jules Ulke. That photo taken with a tripod by the brothers lay undiscovered for nearly a century until found in a library cellar. Also unearthed and of interest was a possible historic picture of the president lying on his deathbed, again taken it seems by one of the Ulke brothers. This is yet to be confirmed, but it does bear an uncanny and striking resemblance to the departed president, does it not? Later, the landlord or someone else would discard one of the bloodstained pillows out of the window and into the street. It seems the landlord would decide later to charge visitors to view the bedroom, minus one of the bloodstained pillows, of course. Some people will do anything for money, won't they?

Later that evening, a Mr William Clerk "the tenant of the room returns and find his room in a shambles. That night he climbed into Lincoln's deathbed and fell asleep under the same coverlet that warmed the body of the dying president."

After leaving the boarding house the deceased president would then be escorted under military guard to the White House and placed in a plain pine box. Someone remarked sarcastically that it resembled a shipping crate but "Lincoln would not have minded, he was always a man of simple tastes."

Then at the White House, the corpse would be removed to the popularly named "Prince of Wales" bedroom to await autopsy by Edward Curtis and Joseph Barnes, both surgeons, of course. Afterwards, it seems that Mrs Lincoln requested a lock of her husband's hair; this would be taken for the grieving widow by one of the attending surgeons and each man would be offered a lock of the president's hair. After President Kennedy's death, his wife Jackie also removed a lock of her husband's hair as a keepsake as he lay in his casket. Then, during the hastily arranged autopsy, that fatal bullet or lead ball would pop out of the mucous, membrane or medulla, then land on a waiting silver dish. Today, it can be seen in a museum in Maryland and there is still some doubt of what the bullet actually weighs. Apparently, after the autopsy, one doctor removed and took home a small fragment of Lincoln's skull and another doctor discovered some blood stains on his shirt, and amazingly both doctors would preserve and revere them later, so much so that they became treasured family heirlooms. This sounds so like Catholicism in their macabre veneration of blood and bones, all very unhealthy and non-Biblical as well. Then later the body would be professionally prepared for open display by paid embalmers.

Performing this task would be Dr Brown, the same technician who had embalmed the president's eleven-year-old son Willie in 1863 after his sudden death of typhoid fever in the Green Room of the White House. It is then decided that Willie's coffin would accompany his father's on the long funeral train journey to Springfield. Before then, Lincoln would be dressed in the same clothes he had chosen to wear for his second inauguration. Someone said he had not worn these clothes since that day on March 4th 1865. Mrs Lincoln did not attend these preparations of her husband's body nor was she present on the slow-moving train to accompany the coffins of her husband and her young son for entombment in the family mausoleum then being prepared in Springfield, being too distraught to leave her darkened White House bedroom. Poor woman, she must have been so emotional and in a fixed state of shock.

Now Edwin M. Stanton will offer "$100,000 REWARD! THE MURDERER of our late beloved President Abraham Lincoln IS STILL AT LARGE." And in his future sights were John Wilkes Booth, John Surratt, his mother Mary and David Herold. But for them and other suspects, the manhunt was on and up and running.

Edwin Stanton needed help. By the third day, it had become obvious that he could not devote his time exclusively to the manhunt, as he had a lot on his mind. He had almost broken down after Lincoln died, but his brain was able to rule his heart. There were other concerns: a war to win. And without Lincoln at his side, Stanton had to go on alone. The new president (Johnson) was not ready to assume the role of commander-in-chief. Stanton had to arrange Lincoln's majestic funeral and then send the body on an unprecedented national tour on the way home to Springfield. I do wonder what sustained him through all of these long hours because he must have also suffered days without sleep and always with some new military or state problem being brought to his office to ponder over and solve. Did he pray, I wonder, for courage and guidance from God? Was he a believer, who knows? But pull through this during the period of mourning for the nation he certainly did. These days, I suggest, would be Edwin Stanton's finest hours, his glory days when he almost ruled America. He died in

1869 aged only fifty-five, the same year that John Wilkes Booth was removed from the secret grave that Edwin Stanton had consigned him to. Four years later, President Johnson ordered John Wilkes Booth' body to be returned to his waiting family, then later being interred in Maryland with the deceased Booth family members.

Many today still visit John Wilkes Booth's grave and place a small stone on its surface for some strange reason, and I know it's a Jewish custom as well. I suspect that few will visit Edwin McMasters Stanton's grave in Washington or know where it is or even care.

In researching this book I have come to have a rather growing admiration and respect for Edwin Stanton, a man I knew nothing about before I started my research on Lincoln or had even heard of. I have none for the others who stood trial except for Anna Surratt and for young Fanny Seward (who died a year later after the terrible events in her family home). Both young ladies never fully recovered emotionally from those events of Good Friday in 1865. I suspect all involved with the assassination of Lincoln were unsaved, but for the born-again Bible-believer, the Judgment Seat of Christ (2 Corinthians 5:10) beckons. All others will be summoned one day to stand before the Great White Throne Judgment as described in the Book of Revelation 20:11-15.

The funeral

At the White House, in the confusing days before the funeral, Edwin M. Stanton watched events unfold, still dispatching his commands, nothing missing his eagle eye. He would prepare and promote Lincoln's funeral with relish, taking it upon himself to perform this task with all the dignity his professionalism could show.

Throughout the long night, carpenters, painters and other journeymen would labour and toil in the White House to erect a seating plan for 600 invited guests. The coffin had now been replaced with a $1,500 mahogany design showcase, that simple packing case consigned elsewhere. The catafalque was assembled from walnut and now stood at 15 feet high with a domed canopy of black silk cloth covering it. On the walls of the East Room, the mirrors were draped in black alpaca and white crepe, a touch of superstition that was common in the day. An impressive sight indeed, but was there a Holy King James Bible on display? We can only hope so.

Bells would later toll and the crowds would gather to file past the open prepared coffin where the president's head lay resting on a white silk pillow.

Supposedly Lincoln on his deathbed

Seen in the crowd of many mourners would be the 22-year-old Captain Robert Lincoln with his 12-year-old brother Tad. "His face swollen with tears, scarlet with bursting chokes," is how a friend of the family remembered him. Earlier, Tad had asked the Navy Secretary: "Oh Mr. Welles, who killed my father?" Mrs Mary Todd Lincoln did not attend the service.

But for now, rehearsed religious rituals from paid church pastors would be heard, along with pitiful recited prayers and empty eulogies. Lincoln was not a religious man. His family were Baptists but it seems, he was a sceptic who naturally kept his views to himself for political reasons. Interestingly, he once remarked that the two books in his log cabin home were the Holy Bible and the collected works of Shakespeare and there's nothing wrong with that, I suggest. During this time of mourning, many ministers in lofty pulpits in Washington, Chicago and New York would falsely equate him with Moses and even Jesus, which is blasphemous!

Of course, many were deeply upset that he should even be in a theatre at all and on "Good Friday" at that. One eloquent pastor put it like this to his parishioners: "Would that Mr. Lincoln had fallen elsewhere than at the very gates of hell, in the theatre to which, through persuasion, he reluctantly went." All seemed to preach and proclaim that Lincoln had been forced to visit the Ford Theatre that night. This is not true. All of them were wrong in their condemnation of Lincoln and his theatre attendance. The man simply wanted to go to take his mind away from the War.

"The Service over, Abraham Lincoln's trip to myth land began," wrote one author. Well, myths have to be manufactured somewhere, don't they, so why not a theatre or concert hall?

Eventually departing the White House, six white horses with black tassels and flounces would carry the hearse to the Capitol rotunda, the coffin was set on a high platform in a case of glass. All the silent and standing spectators would stare as it passed before their eyes. Few would forget this once-in-a-lifetime spectacle as it passed before them in solemn silent splendour.

This was Lincoln's lasting legacy, something I'm sure he would have abhorred.

Finally, under the impressive 180-foot-high rotunda, the murdered president's coffin would be situated on a raised catafalque that, since that day, has been a required stand for each departed president's coffin to be placed for inspection by the public. But now Lincoln's bier will be covered by a canopy revealing a gilt eagle covered with crepe and perhaps some other mysterious religious hieroglyphics symbols on open display.

Such former presidents as Kennedy, Reagan and Eisenhower are three of the ten state ceremonies hosted at the famed rotunda. However, Woodrow Wilson, Franklin Roosevelt, Harry Truman and Richard Nixon all declined this honour for private reasons. I doubt Lincoln would have demanded or desired for a funeral of this magnitude, or for it to be held in his honour. It will be interesting to learn in the future if Barack "Barry" Obama accepts or refuses this honour for his own coffin, or for that matter Donald Trump, or Joe Biden and I think I know the answer to xthese questions.

Once the pomp and ceremony had ceased, the heavy coffin departed for the station to transport the president's body on "the funeral train" to travel on a thousand-mile journey to Springfield, stopping at ten chosen cities on the way and passing through a hundred small towns and hamlets for the waiting public to watch the train steam by. It is estimated an amazing 25 million people who wished to pay their last respects watched the train on its journey, all run with military clockwork precision. Edwin Stanton would accept nothing less, but it was not all over yet.

The final journey

A nine-car rail carriage in no expense funeral train draped in black silk and Hessian (of course) with a large portrait of Lincoln fixed to the front of the engine now awaited at the station for these very important passengers to be delivered. The convoy would be equipped to cater for three hundred people invited along and amongst them, would be a skilled mortician and obliging undertakers all ready to perform their skills with the wax and lipstick and other tricks up their black frock coats. The open coffin was to be viewed at many appointed city stops and displayed in many locations on its journey to Lincoln's final resting place.

Naturally, the decaying corpse would need constant work on the face for the president needs to look as if he were resting, rather like Sleeping Beauty. Thousands of waiting mourners would slowly and silently file past the cadaver at stations and town halls. Mrs Lincoln, it seems, would not be aboard the train. I do wonder if Dr Charles Leale was on board. He was, after all, in the honour guard for Lincoln's body in Washington and I'm sure he would have seen it as his duty to accompany the deceased president to his final resting place. Was Laura Keene perhaps offered a golden ticket for the ride and if so, I hope she did not wear or bring along that blood-soaked dress that she displayed at the Ford Playhouse that fateful Good Friday.

With Lincoln's final arrival into his hometown on May 3rd, his journey had now ended. Yet over the next few years, his body would be moved and relocated many times; there would even be a botched body snatch, can you believe? Later, Mary Todd Lincoln and two of her sons would finally be interred there with her husband. Captain Robert Lincoln would himself be buried at Arlington National Cemetery. I personally suggest the Lincoln monument at Oak Ridge cemetery is way over the top, and I suggest that even good old "Abe" Lincoln would agree with me on this, well, I hope so.

Finally, there is an interesting little mention told in Nigel Blundell and Roger Boar's book *The World's Greatest Ghosts* and it concerns the fabled Lincoln train, so I quote it in full: "President Lincoln's coffin was carried on a special funeral train, which stopped for eight minutes at each station along the route so people could pay their respects. Soon afterwards there were reports of a phantom train. It was draped in black and bore the president's coffin. One carriage carried a band of skeletal musicians. As the ghostly train passed along the funeral route, clocks stopped for exactly eight minutes." Well, make of this what you will!

Meanwhile, after escaping Washington John Wilkes Booth would be joined by a willing accomplice David Herold, with other shadowy conspirators also joining him on the trail. They would eventually be forced to seek medical aid, plus some warm food and shelter wherever they can find it. Once Booth sought fame and fortune; now he was a fugitive being hunted like a sewer rat. Once Booth had basked in thunderous applause and warm adoration, but now he could only fear the shame of being apprehended and caged like a lark and be gawped and pawed at. But for John Wilkes Booth, it may well be his final appearance, later played out at Garrett's farm before an audience of invited soldiers no less. I suspect he had decided he would not be taken alive. But Edwin Stanton, now patiently waiting in his office in Washington for news of Booth's capture, would be sorely disappointed if his quarry was dead. Hadn't his personal hope always been to apprehend and arrest all of those willing conspirators who assisted Booth in the murder of the president and see them swinging from a rope and especially John Wilkes Booth?

However, once in the subdued post-Lincoln Washington era, the police hastily assembled a "dragnet" and Edwin Stanton's fuelled obsession was now in overdrive, locating the other fugitive co-conspirators now under arrest. Also, it should be remembered, "Stanton and others were certain that Booth was merely the agent of a confederate conspiracy." I think he was probably correct in this early assumption of what had happened leading up to the shooting at the Ford Theatre on Friday night. All that was missing so far for Stanton's satisfaction was the capture and arrest of John Surratt as well. If you recall, he disappeared hours after the shooting in the theatre. And it seems that he was offered some important assistance of possible papal protection by the *church fathers* to desert the country. His sick mother, incidentally, was soon to be visited by these priests ministering and praying the rosary with her, as she now festered in a hot prison (much more on Surratt later).

Many others (innocent or not) were being detained as well in most of Stanton's assorted military stockades and elsewhere in the capital. The evidence was often fabricated for those brought to trial and administered at the prepared illegal military court. It must also be remembered that Edwin Stanton was one of the first of Lincoln's cabinet to arrive at his old friend William Seward's home after the failed attempted murder of the old man and there he witnessed that: "The bed was saturated with blood then the rest of the nightmare came into focus: Fanny Seward, wandering like a pale ghost her dress dripping with blood." I suspect this sight of the young girl whom he had known since she was a small child must have affected him more deeply that even he would realise.

The terrible sight and shock of his old friend lying bloodied and wounded on a soaked eiderdown must also have spurred him to track down those wicked men who had perpetrated these deeds on an old Cabinet friend and his innocent young daughter Fanny. They would be punished with the full force of the Government which was now secure in Stanton's safe capable hands.

Incidentally, I have just learned by chance that 12-year-old Tad Lincoln was watching and enjoying the pantomime "Aladdin" at the Grover's Theatre in Washington with his tutor when the terrible news was announced from the stage by the manager that his father had just been shot and perhaps be dead. Poor boy! It seems that all who sat or stood were standing around him could hear his pitiful sobbing in that shocked theatre. He would not be comforted! He was then rushed home to the White House. Sadly, his simple request to be allowed to be taken to the Peterson House to say goodbye to his beloved "Pa" was refused. I wonder who made that cruel and wrong decision. Six years later he himself was dead of tuberculosis. Also on that popular pantomime path was John Wilkes Booth, who would apparently hire a vacant theatre when possible for the coming Christmas season employing hundreds of fellow unemployed actors and musicians during those hungry years of the Civil War, thereby enabling many to earn money for that expensive overrated date in December that has nothing to do with the birth of the Lord Jesus Christ.

Funny enough, one of the most popular productions Booth produced and probably directed himself was that old festive favourite "Aladdin". They say justice is blind, don't they? But it was never true in Edwin Stanton's case. This driven, perhaps demented man who, it seems, at times never slept knew exactly what he desired and demanded of himself and of others who crossed his path in those post-assassination hours. The Secretary of War would now appoint himself as judge and jury in seeking swift justice for the murder for his commander-in-chief and for this he would go that extra-long crooked mile (legal or not) to achieve this. With a hand-picked tribunal aiding him, he would probably succeed (he would argue this not only for himself but also for the Union and for Lincoln, the lost president who would never return). For Secretary of War Edwin M. Stanton, revenge would always be justified and always best served cold from a Hallmark silver platter. "But vengeance is mine, I will repay, saith the Lord." (Romans 12:19). We also learn that "Stanton did not suffer fools. He couldn't." Yet to me he was still very much a principal player in the ongoing open conspiracy concerning Abraham Lincoln's death, and yes, John Wilkes Booth as well, concerning the mystery of whether he was in that barn that night when surrounded by Union soldiers or whether he was miles away, easily escaping to a new life and a new name. These are all unanswered questions that are being exhibited but must finally be exposed one day.

I also learned that, "If any man sat at Lincoln's right hand during the war of rebellion it was Edwin McMasters Stanton." But for now, he was preparing to wage his own private battle on the suspected men and one woman who murdered Abraham Lincoln.

"He was determined to apprehend the criminals," we are informed. But first, there would have to be a trial and its final outcome would be significant in American jurisprudence.

Chapter 3: "The Ghost Train"

As the slain president's "creepy" corpse on display embarked on that sombre and single hometown journey to Springfield, the war-weary nation mourned and waited. Apparently, the corpse travelled on a newly constructed presidential steam engine to be known as the "Dean Richmond". It also boasted a hearse car prepared and fitted with black silk throws and drapes finished with swinging silver tassels and with a paid permanent embalmer and undertaker in continuous residence, preparing the corpse for future viewings by thousands of mourners.

Later, the coffin would be transported by four to six black horses from the train to the many statehouses of the towns and cities for viewing by grieving crowds. A newspaper at the time reported that, "in Chicago queues leading to the city courthouse moved forward one foot an hour". It must have been an amazing sight to behold and be part of, and none would ever forget it for the rest of their lives, I suspect. But, of course, the body cannot be refrigerated between stops to maintain its facial features, so the embalmers in attendance frequently struggled in difficult conditions to somehow make it acceptable for future sightings and display, and not always successfully, we are told because wax can collapse or melt due to the temperature.

The funeral train now began its slow arduous journey westward to its expected destination, and then afterwards to steam into history. It seems that the specially designed and purpose-built carriage that housed Lincoln and son with all its accoutrements was on track. The raised hearse prepared for public viewings would years later be "torched" in a mysterious fire by someone unknown. As the train steamed out of a sombre Washington, we are informed through the press that "the nation can now finally mourn for its fallen but never to be forgotten Commander-in-Chief, Abraham Lincoln." John Wilkes Booth, however, was himself on the move by horse and with a broken leg, which was definitely hindering him in reaching safely to his future destination, known politely then as the 'gallant south.'

Following his escape over the navy yard bridge in Washington, Wilkes Booth had made over thirteen stops along the way, with the most important for him arriving at Dr. Samuel Mudd's home, and in the middle of the night as well. I am proposing that he must have known the way and in the dark as well to reach the doctor's front door. The Mudd residence had been suggested for use in the previous failed attempt to kidnap Lincoln if we are to believe assorted reports. The house was then very much off the main highway, yet Booth and Herold were able to locate it and gain help and assistance once being admitted, it seems. Mudd would later foolishly claim that he had not recognised Wilkes Booth on that fateful night when the two men knocked on his door. This cannot be true because it seems he had in fact met with Booth maybe half a dozen times from 1864 onwards, as far as we know. Booth was apparently seen in Mudd's local catholic church on one occasion.

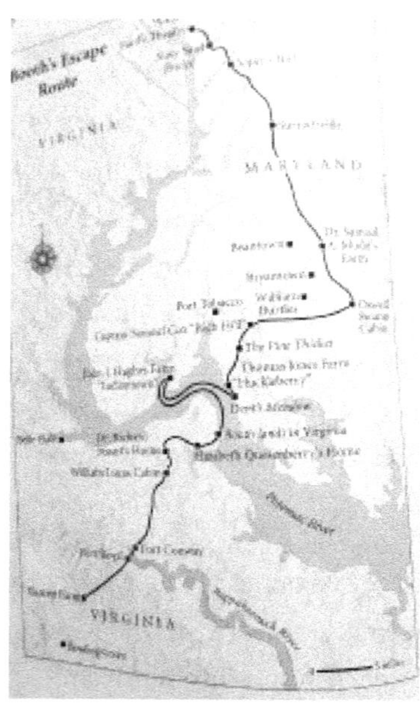

Booth's escape map

In fact, "the court nearly hanged Mudd, his prevarications were painful," as Mr. Fredrick Stone, his defence attorney, remembered some years later when discussing this controversial trial and its final outcome for his client. But arrive at the obliging doctor's front door Booth and Herold finally did and all in the dark as well!

If nothing else, Booth was always persistent in what he demanded. Now, whilst in the doctor's capable hands, his wounded leg would finally be treated by using two panels of wood from a chest drawer because obviously, the doctor had no splints on hand. Later, both men would also be offered shelter and food for the night, then both hopefully to depart the next day.

I do not support the popular assumption that Mudd was just a "good old country doctor" somehow going about his medical business caring for his patients, suddenly shattering his comfortable world when two unknown strangers hammered on his closed door out of the dark in the middle of the night demanding medical aid if you please.

In fact, Samuel Mudd was apparently no longer practising medicine but had turned his hand at working a lucrative 500-acre farm employing over fifty slaves no less. Mudd, I'm afraid, was no emancipator of African-Americans either, but rather despised the idea of giving them their freedom. I think he saw them very much like children to be seen and definitely not heard.

I suggest this pro-Confederate doctor had made the personal acquaintance of Booth the previous year and had been familiarised with Booth's previous preposterous plans to kidnap the president and maybe offered his home to detain the president as an unwilling prisoner, then hopefully to ransom him for thousands of captured Confederate troops.

However, to be fair to the doctor, I'm not sure if he was fully cognisant of the fact that Booth's future plans for the president meant shooting him. Booth had only made this fateful decision on the morning of Good Friday, and there is no way he could have brought the doctor into the picture of what he was about to perform with a derringer pistol several hours later in the Ford theatre, unless of course, Booth dispatched a messenger with a letter to Mudd asking for sanctuary after the murder, then explaining to Mudd what he performed in the crowded Ford Theatre. But this scenario seems unlikely to me.

At this point, some consideration has to be made of a 1924 book entitled *The suppressed truth about the assassination of Abraham Lincoln* by Burke McCarthy. The author argues: "That Booth, as a secret convert to Roman Catholicism, had killed Lincoln in obedience to the demands of Jesuit plotters." The author also states that a Rear Admiral George A. Baird who had been on the "Montauk" when Booth's body was later identified and that he had seen naval officers take a small Roman Catholic medal from the dead man's neck... this it seems later disappeared."

I can smell a Jesuit aroma swirling around here perhaps!

Coincidently as I write this it is very near to the anniversary of the actual capture and shooting of John Wilkes Booth on April 25th, 1865. But there are, in my opinion, too many disparities that do not add up in the official published report of what was played out that night at Garrett's farm.

So, I humbly offer the official version and the unofficial version for your perusal:

John Wilkes Booth and fellow co-conspirator David Herold were finally located in hiding at Richard Garrett's farm on

April 25th. There, they were eventually cornered like rats in the farm's tobacco curing barn. Also, do you remember that unexplained mysterious password that Booth offered to the enquiring sentry on the navy bridge? And how he was surprisingly allowed to leave the "locked down" town when all the other bridges were heavily guarded and closed for all traffic? But not this particular bridge. That password was of course "TBR". So, was this an oblique reference somehow to the mysterious Tobacco Road that, once uttered by Booth, eventually led him to the tobacco curing shed on the Garrett spread near Port Talbot Virginia?

Once there, the accused were surrounded by excited shouting Union soldiers who had strict orders from Edwin Stanton to bring Booth back alive for future questioning, hopefully, to stand trial later with the other suspects. But for some unknown reason, one of the soldiers at the besieged barn, a 43-year-old Sergeant Boston Corbett, who was remembered as "a religious eccentric" by his pals for some reason, took it upon himself to step forward and aim his gun at Wilkes Booth, mortally wounding him. He would then later declare to his commanding officer when asked, why he went against strict orders not to fire: "Sir, God Almighty directed me." He certainly had taken aim at Booth (or someone) through the flames of the wooden ventilation slats of the barn, hitting him in the spine and bringing him down that day.

Sgt. Boston Corbett

Booth was now seriously wounded. Now, I don't know about you, but somehow Corbett fits the profile of a Jack Ruby plant in this melodrama dramatically staged on the farm. Booth, or someone like him, was then dragged clear of the smouldering barn and propped up against a tree.

Entering into the drama was the live-in school tutor to the Garrett children, she is a Miss Lucinda Holloway. She decided to take it upon herself to have Booth gently moved to the covered porch of the farmhouse. I don't suppose she attempted this herself but enlisted some of the soldiers for this mercy task.

Once there she then placed a pillow under his head and stayed with him until he expired.

For the rest of her life, it seems this lady would remember his face as being "luminous… tenderly. Lucinda Holloway will massage his temples and forehead. Her fingertips felt the life draining out of him. The pulsation in his temples grew weaker and weaker until extinction descends on the dying man."

This description of the ministering angel reads as a chapter lifted out of a Georgette Heyer novel (and no disrespect to this fine author, now deceased). It seems the young lady would then recall this scene with relish in the long years ahead of her and recount it often to whoever requested it of her. Later, she would also secretly remove a lock of Booth's hair for herself and also gain his field glasses, "his prized possession", of course. They seem to have performed this saved lock hair procedure very much in those days, didn't they? Remember Stanton using his pocket scissors to perform the same task for the Secretary of the Navy's wife? Then there was Mrs Lincoln's mournful request for a souvenir lock of her husband's hair, which should not be forgotten either.

The dying man now slumped forward on the crowded porch, held in the warm arms of Miss Holloway, departing from this fallen world and en route for hell. Then, Booth was heard to whisper to no one, in particular, those mysterious words: "Useless, useless." Then the man was gone. Once he boasted some years previously that: "I have too great a soul to die like a criminal." Ah, the arrogance of men and never a sincere word, it seems, of repentance from this arrogant actor. So often the case from many a dying person's parched fading lips. For him, or "someone", it is now the final curtain of his life. But is it because: "The hour is coming in the which all that are in the graves shall hear his voice" (John 5:28).

This should be of concern to all unsaved people!

I wonder: Was the young impressionable Lucinda Holloway his final loving fan? Did she perhaps descend into a deep mourning soon afterwards as these events that changed her young life? Did she perhaps attempt to acquire an autograph from him to add to her other mementoes? It seems she never committed to marriage and I wonder why because it cannot be for the lack of suitors. So, was it perhaps her that placed that suspect religious medallion with loving care around his neck (a saint Christopher, in fact)? He, if you didn't know or care, is the so-called catholic patron saint of travellers.

(For some reason unknown, in 1970 Paul VI, downgraded this popular saint if indeed he ever existed. But who cares anyway!)

Later, when Booth's diary was discovered by searching Union troops and handed over to Edwin Stanton, it seems eighteen pages had been mysteriously removed. Also retrieved from Wilkes Booth's personal belongings were five professionally posed "pin-up" pictures of assorted young ladies tucked neatly into his leather wallet. Sadly it seems Mrs Mary Surratt was not one of them to grace Booth's pocket book. I suspect Miss Holloway or maybe Mrs Surratt were the last two ladies to see him alive because someone offered him this useless religious trinket which he accepted. Both ladies have to be considered as possibly offering Booth that mysterious medallion or placing it tenderly around his neck. But then maybe doctor Mudd or his wife performed that role, for whatever bizarre purpose. I suppose the jury is still out on this one.

Another popular theory:

John Wilkes Booth the actor had a tenuous connection, it seems, to the then Vice President Johnson. Indeed, he paid a courteous call earlier at the Kirkwood House hotel, where Johnson was then in residence, just hours in fact before the shooting of Lincoln. Once there, in the lobby of the hotel he left one of his calling cards with the desk clerk which reads cryptically: "Don't wish to disturb you, are you in?" This card was left in Johnson's hotel mailbox, all very strange.

Later, Mrs Lincoln, always a shrewd judge of politicians and their personal greedy motives, was always suspicious of "good old Andy" Johnson and his possible role in her husband's murder. She also made her views known as well in most of the polite Washington social circles about him.

Now, into this post-assassination period of mourning Washington chief of police, a Colonel Lafayett C. Baker appeared. A "secret service melodramist in the first order," remembered one of his old working colleagues concerning Baker and not with affection, it seems.

More importantly to me is that Baker was apparently one of Stanton's favourites. It seems that Baker had somehow made the acquaintance of some of the conspirators and probably Booth. So, was Baker the "points man" involved somehow in

Booth's dramatic escape over that bridge just hours after the shooting, using that ambiguous password which has never been explained? Later, after the "body" of Booth was returned to Washington it would be Baker who would take command of the body and its disposal. It appears that no photographs were taken of Booth's body or at least none that have survived. Later, the corpse would, in fact, be interred in the old arsenal yard, where it would be placed secretly in a plain wooded box, then left in an unmarked location.

Incidentally, the other four hanged conspirators would themselves later be placed in that same hidden plot. It seems all five Booth conspirators now lay side-by-side for the next few years hidden away from the public eye. Yet, "For there is nothing hid which shall not be manifested" (Mark 4:22).

It has also been suggested by some researchers of this painful period that Wilkes Booth was involved with the then Vice President Johnson in some form of collusion to remove Lincoln as president, thereby opening the White House door for Johnson to succeed him as the 17th president. This suggestion mainly arrives from that enigmatic visiting card measuring just 3 inches by 2 inches that Booth had left for Johnson at the Kirkwood House. I'm not sure this is enough evidence to point the actor's finger solely at Johnson. I suggest a well-oiled cabal with or without Johnson's support was active plotting Lincoln's demise. The Kirkwood was, of course, where the VP could be found with his retinue and other dubious freeloaders working and playing hard. It could be that Johnson's then secretary and confidant Colonel William A. Browning was the crucial points man liaising with Booth and other nefarious parties hoping to gain financially from the coming collapse of the defeated Confederacy.

Both Booth and Browning were not strangers, it seems, as they became acquainted with each other in 1844 in Nashville. Apparently, both Booth and Johnson got along "splendidly," even sharing assorted mistresses, it seems, bringing, of course, all the disgusting sexually transmitted diseases to those who dabble in this perversion of the body. Remember, continued and repeated debauchery will eventually lead to death, leading all unrepentant sinners to the fires of a waiting hell, where the worm never dies. Terrible but true to contemplate or to consider for all unsaved lost souls!

Browning died in 1866 and strangely enough Mrs Lincoln confided to a close friend, Miss Sally Ore, that "Johnson had some hand in this." Maybe the grieving widow knew something we don't know, and it seems odd as well that Johnson apparently never sent Mrs Lincoln a note of condolence after her husband's murder, which is sad and strange. She certainly thought so!

All of these important politicians could have been members of a Masonic manoeuvre to remove Lincoln. Of course, there had been several earlier calls and attempts to kill Lincoln, he being a very unpopular man to many Americans tired of the never-ending War. Most of the Masons of that period would or could have been attending that infamous Washington Lodge, which could well have been Jesuit-infiltrated and controlled by papal Rome and still flourishing today under the Jesuit pope.

Andrew Johnson was certainly a Mason, it seems, having been initiated in 1851. As regards Colonel Lafayette Baker, he was another practising lodge man. More interestingly, the colonel was running ex-Confederate spies and perhaps one of many as well, with one in particular interest, this being James William Boyd. Boyd had been employed successfully in the past by the colonel for clandestine purposes. And doesn't he bear a similar likeness to Booth, I suggest (see pictures below), sporting the same initials as well. It seems that Baker had obtained some "dirt" on Boyd and would use it when he needed information on an enemy rather like a workshop vice.

Stanton had also suspiciously had Boyd brought from prison before the assassination of Lincoln. Perhaps Boyd will be briefed and paid to impersonate Booth, but of course, being unaware that it will be him who will be later shot dead by Sergeant Corbett in the barn, allowing, of course, Booth to escape Stanton's justice in Washington.

Booth, left, Boyd, right

Some days after the assassination, Booth had departed with ease from Washington and perhaps with Johnson's valuable assistance and was now free. With Johnson's support, Baker sent James W. Boyd to join up with Booth and Herold on the escape trail. Yet Booth and Herold were later cornered in Garrett's tobacco shed when the Union soldiers, under the command of a lieutenant Harmon P. Norris, the husband coincidently of Stanton's niece, quickly surrounded the barn and ordered the barn to be lit, thereby hoping to force out the fugitives and into his custody.

Yet Herold quickly ran and shouted to Norris, "That's not Booth in there". Only later after intense interrogation would he change his story. I suggest a likely liaison point for the three men "to hook up" would be in the notorious Port Tobacco. I appreciate how the journalist George Alfred Townsend described the town after a visit and he writes: "If any place in the world is utterly given over to depravity it is Port Tobacco...gambling, corner fighting, and shooting matches were its lyceum education and he compared it with the slimy river and adjacent swamps of the great reptile period when iguanodons and pterodactyls and pliosaurs ate each other.

Into this abstract of Gomorrah, the few detectives looking for Booth and Herold went like angels who visited Lot. It should also be remembered that co-conspirator George Azterodt, who had failed in murdering Andrew Johnson at the Kirkwood, was associated with this venue, and he actually went by the nickname of "Port Tobacco" where beer and bourbon, we are informed, flowed like water. A likely location for the three men to choose this town of sexual proclivities and assorted perversities, making even Casanova blush, it seems.

As regards those still searching Union troops, the manhunt was at a standstill. In other words, the trail had gone cold, well for the time being anyway. Port Tobacco, it must be remembered, was an important rebel stronghold then. I'm sure John Surratt would have been a frequent visitor to the town as well, perhaps sampling the open wares of the flesh. The town would also offer methods of sharpening the spying skills that he had used previously in his mother's drinking tavern/post office in Surrattsville before his dismissal.

Interestingly, four years later President Andrew Johnson granted permission by executive order for John Wilkes Booth's body (or someone's) to be removed and interred in the family plot in Baltimore. The same instruction was also offered to the other conspirators, with their respective families accepting this offer and claiming their bodies for reburial.

But remember, "Jesus said," Verily, Verily I say unto thee, except a man be born again, he cannot see the Kingdom of God" (John 3:3-7). You have been warned!

Colonel Baker would later in 1866 be dismissed by President Johnson, for personal reasons. He died in 1868, supposedly of meningitis or being possibly murdered by persons unknown with arsenic poisoning no less, this according to a laboratory analysis performed later on a sample of Baker's hair obtained in the 1970s. All very strange indeed, but then the whole Lincoln saga has left more questions unanswered than answered, it seems.

However, I still suggest there was a tenuous connection between Port Tobacco (TBR), which may be a secret code for Tobacco Road, and that final shootout at the tobacco curing shed at Garrett's farm in Virginia, where supposedly Booth or someone was shot by Corbett, by the same manner in which Lincoln was wounded in the head, directly behind the left ear. And don't forget: he acted against strict army orders. Boston Corbett was never punished for shooting Booth, but he did enjoy an additional compensation, that being fame. The public then celebrated him as "Lincoln's Avenger".

Boston Corbett later received a considerable share in Stanton's reward money, being offered $17,500, the same amount as Lafayette Baker. In fact, the president's own annual salary in those days was a mere $25,000, so not a bad day's work for both gentlemen, it seems.

Strangely enough, Boston Corbett later entered into a private correspondence with the Booth family according to Booth's sister, Asia Booth Clarke. In her later memoirs, she writes: "For by his shot he saved our brother from an ignominious death. May he have no regret." Very kind and forgiving, I thought, from the good lady. As regards the self-mutilation stories about Corbett, I believe they originated from the" dirty tricks" department, hoping to discredit his supposed Christian beliefs that were then espoused to the public.

The old "switcheroo" as they used to refer to it in those good old black-and-white westerns of long ago if you remember, which I certainly do.

In fact, at a hidden location somewhere along that suspicious escape trail Booth now rested with Herold and had newspapers and food brought to him by sympathiser Thomas Jones. It seems Booth enjoyed reading about the hunt for himself in newspaper reports but seemed very disappointed about the public's adulation heaped upon the dead president's memory, with him now cast as the villain. It is important to remember that Lincoln was deeply unpopular because of the War and to date was the only American president to wage a war on his own people.

Booth may also have been waiting for further orders from someone in Washington regarding where he should go next. Later, Booth and Herold were joined by Captain James William Boyd, one of Lafayette Baker's numerous agents, you may remember. It's not clear if the fugitives recognised Boyd or what his future purpose would be. Yet, Booth would later shave off his trademark moustache, maybe at Mudd's obliging house, so he must have been aware that something was being planned concerning his escape. Yet the body recovered from the burning barn and viewed later did boast a moustache and offered protruding sandy red hair as well. But Booth had black hair, so something is wrong!

After all this, perhaps Booth escaped, aided by who knows whom and was quickly reunited with his waiting wife Izola, then journeying in comfort to Canada and seen later in

London. He was also spotted in Bombay of all places. It seems he may even have journeyed to Rome, to meet and personally report to the Jesuit black pope Peter Jan Beckx, or maybe even to have an audience with the pontiff himself, bringing a letter of introduction from John Surratt Jr. (the once Catholic seminary student) who allowed his own mother to hang at the end of a rope. He was now, it seems, comfortably domiciled in Rome under the protection of the "holy mother church," having originally been aided by a senior member of the catholic Jesuit clergy in Montreal. Then in the years to follow Wilkes Booth would use assorted aliases, John R. Wilkes amongst others, very clever indeed.

In 1903, one member of Booth's family would claim through an affidavit that their brother did survive, then later visited and stayed with members of the family ten days at a house in Maryland. So, it seems possible that Booth, if he did escape, lived out another 38 stress-free years, somehow beating the system.

I did come across a strange quote from someone who knew the Booth family and they remembered: "That the Booths had an inherited strain of darkness in them." Not sure what that means. I am perhaps leaning towards the suggestion that Booth did eventually escape and survived as a possible important spy of Andrew Johnson or Colonel Baker, then provided with the necessary letters of transit and money, of course, to pursue his future lifestyle. I'm sure John Wilkes Booth thought of everything concerning himself and his survival. These sorts of people usually do, don't they? But then as an actor of his magnitude, he could perform any role offered him, even understudying the pope and that mysterious black pope if required.

The famed American photographer Alexander Gardner (1821-1882) should also be brought into the picture (sorry for the pun). This Scotsman had indeed previously photographed Lincoln and Albert Pike and in his full wicked Masonic regalia. (Incidentally, if you have inherited any such items from dead Masonic relatives, burn them now!) These two men were just two of the dignitaries Gardener "snapped". He also lugged his heavy camera onto the battlefield, capturing some historic scenes of that civil war, later photographing events in and around Lincoln's final train journey home to Springfield.

This now leads me to the fact that Gardner was himself a practising Mason and Mormon and socialist, and oddly enough, after "retiring", in 1871 this famed photographer founded an insurance company aptly named *The Masonic Mutual Relief Ass Ins. Company*. This certainly seems to me quite an occupation change to pursue midlife. Certainly, other famed photographers of the past, such as Adams, Bresson, Avedon, and Karsh, never (as far as I know) considered such a drastic life change but rather continued using their talent well into old age, and to great success.

Alexander Gardener remains perhaps the best-remembered man to ever capture on camera those iconic scenes of the execution by hanging of the four conspirators on that hot day in 1845 (these will naturally be featured later). He was also called upon to record pictures or present evidence of John Wilkes Booth's naked body when his corpse was laid out on a long narrow table under a huge canopy deck of the ship USS Montauk, this being performed on Edwin Stanton's orders. It seems that twelve handpicked men would be a part of a mock inquest that would formally identify Boyd's body as that of Booth's.

Several witnesses reluctantly brought on board to identify the deceased had some serious doubts that this was indeed the body of the late unlamented John Wilkes Booth. None seemed surprised that the face had a moustache because none had been informed earlier that Booth had apparently shaved his moustache off on Easter Sunday. Brought on board was Dr. John Franklin May who had previously removed a neck growth on Booth. When presented with the corpse on the ship, he replied: "There's no resemblance in that corpse to Booth, nor can I believe it to be him". This physician was then the coerced (probably by Lafayette Baker), only to be finally dismissed. Indeed, soon after viewing the corpse on display, many others expressed their own personal doubts as well. This definitely was not the John Wilkes Booth that they had known and worked with previously.

Earlier on board that moored ship, some of the detained prisoners would surprisingly be primed, posed, and photographed for public consumption, namely Sam Arnold, Michael Olaughlin, and Edmund Spangler, but not Dr. Samuel Mudd for some strange reason. Also photographed were Lewis Payne, George Atzerodt, and David Herold, all posed by Gardner for his camera but not Mrs Mary Surratt, surprisingly. I'm not sure why she was spared Gardner's superb vista of vision in capturing her striking facial features. Those finished

Booth corpse pictures that he had taken soon afterwards mysteriously vanished "almost as soon as they were taken and have never been seen again," recalled one historian of that period.

The mock inquest would then formally identity Boyd's body as that of Booth. I suspect those wet-plate pictures must be somewhere today, just waiting for some keen Lincoln or Booth researcher to locate their whereabouts, possibly filed away under some other name or occasion.

Did Edwin Stanton have them deliberately destroyed, perhaps himself smashing those photographic" wet plates" in a seething Stanton strop as he looked at the face of the man who had caused him so much pain and grief? He was also very angry that photographs of Lincoln's corpse had been allowed to be taken on that funeral train.

Amazingly, just one photograph previously taken by Gardener of the dead Lincoln has survived, being discovered a few years ago, tucked away in a locked museum vault. As with all of Gardener's wonderful atmospheric photographs, the clarity he captures and the technique he pioneered is brilliant, and these must be his lasting heritage.

But I do wonder why he invested such detail and effort in promoting these almost "timeless" photographs of some of these captured co-conspirators. Or were they intended to be just trophy pictures to be passed around the lodge by smutty men? But for whose enjoyment and why? It's still a mystery, yet Booth's path and Gardener's may just have crossed previously through their blasphemous Masonic rituals or perhaps at those popular theatrical soirées always celebrated backstage after a final theatrical performance. Maybe Gardener even took some of those photographs of the ladies featured in Booth's wallet, who knows.

Now, the story gets more bizarre because in 1878 a young ambitious Mississippi lawyer by the name of Finis L. Bates first encountered a dying man named John St Helen declining on his sick bed, or so Bates thought. The man then proceeded to inform Bates in a so-called deathbed confession that his true name was John Wilkes Booth, that he had previously been a paid agent for President Andrew Johnson, and that he had carried out the assassination of President Lincoln in 1865. The dying man then sobbed with much emotion to Bates, whispering through tears that: "He had killed the best man who ever lived". It seems the man also had important information about that mysterious password that allowed him to cross unfettered over the navy yard bridge to freedom. According to the dying man, this had earlier been given to the guards, it seems, by a mysterious captain who had ridden up previously and instructed the soldiers to offer any stranger immediate access over the bridge, but only if they used this important password.

So, who was this suspicious captain? And was he perhaps hastily dispatched from Andrew Johnson or someone else offering aid to the escaping man? Also, the dying man could recite pages of Shakespeare to Finis Bates and seemed to know much more about what happened in those twelve days as he escaped from Union soldiers. There was also a strong facial resemblance between Booth and George as seen in photographs of that period.

It seems also that in India the fugitive Booth, for some reason, would fake his own death, perhaps in a planned drowning accident on the murky River Ganges of all places. As a convincing actor, it must have worked a charm for him in convincing local authorities of his demise and issuing a death certificate. I rather like to speculate that he perhaps journeyed to beautiful Switzerland and easily faked his own death there perhaps at the famous Reichenbach falls, as another fictional favourite of mine did to perfection so many years ago, courtesy of Arthur Conan Doyle, of course.

It appears that the actor would later return, perhaps for financial or health reasons, to the United States. Once there, he was now comfortable using the new names of John St Helen or David E. George. There is also a report that after he had married and later informed his bride that he was, in fact, Wilkes Booth and not the alias he had long been using, the shocked bride marched him down to the courthouse and insisted he sign the marriage certificate as John Wilkes Booth, which he did, incredibly. Remember that the marriage license is the one license that never expires.

Then years later living under the assumed name of David E. George, this gentleman committed suicide in 1903 by arsenic poisoning in Enid, Oklahoma in the Grand Avenue Hotel, room number four, it seems.

Oh, by the way, remember that lone soldier who shot Booth (or someone) at Garrett's farm, Sergeant Boston Corbett? Well, he is apparently buried in Enid, Oklahoma in an unmarked grave!

After the death of George or Booth, Finis Bates had the body preserved and mummified for posterity and more importantly for financial reasons, of course. It seems there was still an outstanding reward for the body of Booth.

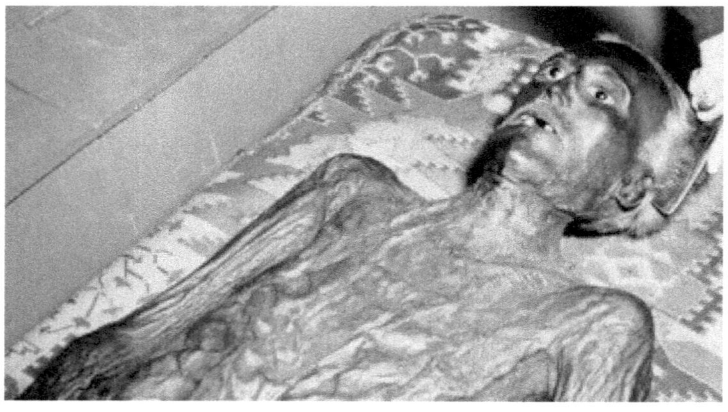

The purported corpse of Booth

Over the years, this gruesome cadaver would be displayed in fairs, circuses and rodeos. Ownership of it would change frequently and many times, until it disappeared somewhere in the 1970s, perhaps into someone's private collection. All very gruesome and also reminiscent of Cromwell's head which also did the financial rounds throughout England!

If the original derringer pistol handled by Booth at the Ford Theatre was stolen in the 1960s, as is claimed, then maybe that same pistol is residing in the same private collector's possession and now posed in the hand of John Wilkes Booth's mummy, to be seen in a spot-lighted glass-sealed cabinet, on view for by invited visitors. All very gruesome, I suggest.

Today, 22 members of the Wilkes Booth family have finally hoped to have the body of their infamous relative exhumed from his supposed grave in Maryland and to have DNA samples collected to settle this question once and for all. But this legal outcome seems to have been stalled in the courts for some legal reason.

Lois Trebisacci, she being Wilkes Booth's great, great, great granddaughter, said in an interview: "I just feel we have the right to know who's buried there." And you know I somehow agree with that enquiring lady. So let's throw some light on this mystery once and for all. But you know what, I'm not holding my breath any time soon.

Chapter 4: "Arrests And Trial Of The Co-Conspirators"

Edwin Stanton's "show trial" was to be performed behind military walls (naturally), and with a supporting cast headed by nine distinguished decorated generals, no less. Amazingly, only one apparently had qualified as a lawyer, that being Lew Wallace of "Ben Hur" fame. In the meantime, Colonel Lafayette Baker's police force had been active in the arrests department as well. By now, most (if not all) of the so-called Lincoln co-conspirators were detained under lock and key waiting for a pre-trial hearing.

Eight suspects had been previously hooded and escorted into the grim old arsenal penitentiary known today as Fort Leslie J. McNair. Only four would apparently leave its stone walls alive. Edwin Stanton, it seems, had laid down 28 strict rules to be observed concerning the prisoners' welfare. Only later would he give permission for young Anna Surratt to occupy the cell next to her ailing mother Mary to care for her; so the man did appear to have some compassion after all. Before then, some of the confused and cowering prisoners would later be re-housed at the "Pen," as it was popularly known. They had earlier been escorted to the ironclad naval vessel, the USS Montauk, where they patiently waited their fate, maybe some even prayed.

Conventionally berthed alongside is The Saugus. In fact, both naval vessels were now to be used as holding pens for processing the prisoners' personal details.

Strangely enough, President Lincoln and his wife Mary had been invited to visit the Montauk, courtesy of the captain, on the afternoon of that terrible day of the assassination. There "the president informed his wife that they must try to be happy again, perhaps to travel, maybe move to Chicago where he would practice his trade again. Freed from the vexation and fear of war and its sister death." Or even maybe a spiritual journey to Jerusalem that he had hoped to visit someday. Maybe once there perhaps to assimilate his confused religious ideas.

Some who knew Lincoln claimed he was a believer in the blood of Christ for the atonement of sin. Others claimed that "he did not believe in the divinity of Christ," wrote one of his biographers. But it was not to be, of course. Within 24 hours, Abraham Lincoln was history.

An interesting observation worth mentioning from the Australian writer Thomas Keneally that I came across recently suggests that, "It is obvious that Lincoln and Mary Todd Lincoln were complicated and fretful souls. Lincoln seems to have been a sometimes acute depressive whereas Mary exhibited a bipolar volatility." Well, I suggest this could be true of any of our world leaders and their wives today because we know almost nothing about their personal lives except through the rumour mill and gossip columns. Of course, that same logic can be applied to all the pagan popes, past and present. I also include the ecumenical and interfaith clerical clowns who parade in ridiculous hats and garish vestments as well!

Back in 1865, arriving on that good ship "Montauk" was Mr. Alexander Gardener, apparently Lincoln's favourite photographer. He then began to open his collapsible tripod. Afterwards, once on board the ship, he would take multiple images of Samuel Arnold, Michael O'Laughlin, Edmond Spangler, George Atzerodt and little Davy Herold, all willing Booth co-conspirators, or so the court would be informed, now held under military detention.

This photographer, it seems, would not have a booked appointment with Mary Surratt, which is interesting to me. With her striking features, he could have made her facial features a work of art to be revealed in glorious monochrome. I can only speculate of why the widow was excluded from this Scotsman's probing lens, possibly because she was then being held in the old capitol prison before being transferred to the "Pen". Or were there other covert reasons we know nothing about?

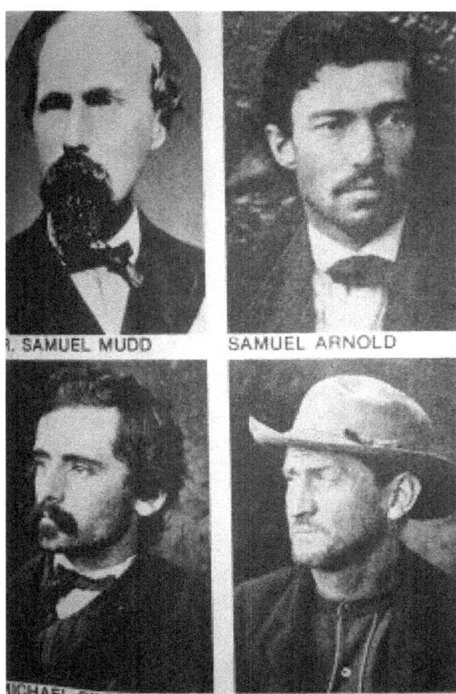

R. SAMUEL MUDD
SAMUEL ARNOLD
MICHAEL O'LAUGHLIN
EDWARD SPANGLER

Grim mug shots of Lincoln's infamous killers and assailants

It seems there were reports of the above widow and others being transported in and around the capitol blindfolded. This may have been some early form of selective disorientation being practised and obviously under Edwin Stanton's orders. This man thought of everything, of course, to add to the prisoners' already noticeable pain and discomfort. So, I doubt Gardener would have refused a rare opportunity to photograph this "infamous" photogenic lady whose name and reputation were all over Washington's newspapers. But who knows? Maybe some lost wet plates of Surratt's image are somewhere and still preserved just waiting to be located. These posed portraits of the male prisoners viewed even today are, in my opinion, some of the most detailed ever recorded of suspects at that time or since.

In these photographs, we can see the suspects posed, with or without handcuffs, and with the ship hulk used as a striking background. However, Mary Surratt is not included. Interestingly, in one of the wanted posters, one of the suspects is pictured in handcuffs. Yet, according to the wanted poster issued at the time, he was still being sought by the police? Um! Someone slipped up there. It would later be quietly withdrawn.

Later, the prisoners were escorted under a military guard to the Old Arsenal Prison (now demolished) in Washington. There, they would be manacled in so-called heavy wrist irons or painful "Lilly irons," as they were then known and remembered. These irons would be secured on the prisoners' hands and measured about 10 inches apart with additional foot chains also used to add to the discomfort (not used on Mrs Mary Surratt, however). Then, and I'm not sure on whose orders, disgusting and suffocating heavy canvas hoods would be added to the torture endured by prisoners as they were placed on shaking perspiring heads (again, not on Mrs Surratt's head or maybe Dr. Mudd's either, it has been suggested).

After being detained and documented, the prisoners would be appropriately housed in their respective cells. Mrs Mary Surratt was placed in cell 153, George Atzerodt (the reluctant assassin) in cell 151, Dr. Samuel Mudd in cell 194, Samuel Arnold in cell

205, Lewis Payne (Paine) in cell 157, Michael O'Laughlin in cell 207, and Edward Spangler in cell 184 with David Herold locked in cell 155. Also being housed in cell 212 in that same grim establishment and as a possible future bargaining chip was skull-and-bones member Mr Burton N. Harrison who had acted as secretary to Confederate President Jefferson Davis. Edwin Stanton always suspected that old Jefferson Davis was deeply involved somehow in the Lincoln plot, and he may have been correct in this assumption, as so much of Davis and his involvement is still unclear.

The prisoners "will be subjected to excessive physical torture while confined to prison awaiting their trial." The men would be forcibly placed in those heavy suffocating canvas hoods to prevent suicide, we are informed. Lewis Powell had attempted this earlier when continually banging his head against a brick wall until restrained. The hoods also were fitted with rope ties allowing only a hole for breathing and eating. Heavy lead weights were fitted over the eye space of these suffocating hoods. Naturally, this caused cruel discomfort to all eye movement. On reflection, this seems to me an early form of sensory deprivation, but Mary Surratt was not subjected to this torture, I do wonder why.

You know it all reminds me of those Muslim suspects detained some years ago in those distinctive orange jumpsuits in camp X in Guantanamo Bay; according to the Bush Government, this was apparently legal. Of course, there are many levels of torture and pain that these prisoners may have also been subjected to repeatedly in their cells that we do not know about, for instance, not being able to see what was happening in and around them even though they could certainly hear what was being said about them in the crudest manner. I suspect there was punching, prodding and pinching from the mocking guards and the usual indignities they must have experienced when using basic toilet facilities, probably buckets when provided. Also, many crude, cruel and cutting remarks must have been used on them for the amusement of the guards. Apparently, one of the men even requested a Holy Bible but this was apparently denied him, and who could or would have read it to him anyway? But Quran's were of course allowed!

As regards Mrs Surratt's genuine state of anxiety as reported to the court by her defence attorney, it seems the lady was suffering serious menopausal problems and frequently requested some pain relief, personally asking to consult a woman doctor if possible. Naturally, this was refused her. It seems that "Mary Surratt's cell consisted of a very thin straw mattress, and an old army blanket and an old pail. She had neither washing utensils nor a chair to sit in nor a single comfort for her toilet or dress, the cell had a cold stone floor later because of this treatment Mrs Surratt began to haemorrhage." Naturally, the judges, all men, were unconcerned about her female plight and why would they be? This discomfort, as far as they were concerned, would be further punishment for her personal role in aiding the fugitive John Wilkes Booth to escape Washington that night after escaping to the sanctuary of her tavern in the suburbs.

Judges at Lincoln's murder trial

"Stanton it seems had the imagination of a torturer," remembered one of his cabinet colleagues years later. That statement would be repeated by the prison physician Dr. George Loring Porter, who wrote to the prison authorities with great concern saying, "that the constant pressure of those thickly padded hoods may induce insanity." I think this good doctor was correct in his medical prognosis in his humane concern about the suffering of those untried prisoners. Of course, doctors have seen it all and heard it all, haven't they? But it just goes with the job.

As regards Edwin Stanton's supposed taste for sadism, wouldn't he have just been a willing participant for the cruel Spanish Inquisition prepared and praised by those wicked Roman Catholic Dominican priests now burning in hell!

After much thought, I have to admit that I do believe Mary Surratt was guilty and some of the other prisoners were all guilty by association in collaborating with Wilkes Booth in what he was about to do in executing Lincoln. Yet it seems to me that after Wilkes Booth learned the electrifying news from Henry Clay Ford that the Lincolns would be at his theatre that evening, nothing or nobody could restrain him. Mary Surratt seems to have gotten pretty close to him in the crucial hours leading up to the shooting of Lincoln. I can only speculate also that Booth confided in her of what he was about to commit in the theatre that Friday evening.

I also suggest that Stanton did believe this also, in that she did know what her matinee idol Wilkes Booth was about to perform in the Ford Theatre that night. This was why he would demand the death penalty for her when the guilty sentence was predictably announced. Later, when Booth finally arrived in a fever of pain at Surrattsville, she was there waiting and watching and anxious, of course, to learn if he had succeeded in murdering Lincoln.

To me, John Wilkes Booth seems to have been badly prepared for the expected hazardous journey he was supposedly about to undertake. So, was he perhaps with some other co-conspirators expecting to be safely holed up in a Washington "safe house" for a few days, then to head off to the south if things went wrong (which of course they did)?

And was it a wise move, I suggest, after the cowardly shooting of Lincoln to launch himself fifteen feet from the box onto a hard wooden stage!?

However, back to the trial hastily summoned by the military, which has to be judged as illegal, certainly by the legal ethics of today that I have seen. These prisoners were under a wrongful jurisdiction of the military; this certainly infringed their civilian status. We now know also that they were prevented from offering evidence on their own behalf, nor were they offered enough time to allow their defence lawyers to prepare a case for the court to consider, which was what Stanton wanted all along.

This was a wrong judicial decision, but Edwin "Czar" Stanton claimed or persuaded the Judge Advocate General Joseph Holt – the chief prosecutor in the trial – that the Union was technically still at war with the South. But I don't think Holt needed much "friendly" persuasion on this matter in going along with Stanton's wishes. In other words, in times of war, civilian courts can be overridden and suspended. In this demand, Stanton seems to have been supported by the then Advocate General and President Andrew Johnson.

I'm not sure how reluctant these gentleman and the court were with regard to its planned and expected outcome, yet they seemed to have gone along with what was expected of them. They also had not seen Booth's damaged diary for court inspection and were probably unaware of its content. I suggest, however, that Johnson was content for many reasons with this legal farce to proceed under Stanton's strict orders and to arrive at its expected outcome.

Of course, it was also expected by many observers and reporters that Mrs Surratt would, once the guilty announcement was made, perhaps serve a life sentence. On the other hand, Mrs Surratt may have been used as a tempting prosecution bait by Edwin "Mars" Stanton in hopefully luring her weak son John to voluntarily return and stand alongside the other accused co-conspirators. Surely Stanton would have argued that this son would not let his own mother hang at the end of a Hessian rope, well, would he?

It seems John Surratt did just that, with the complicity of the catholic church, can you believe? The little rat bolted for a hideaway hole in the nearest catholic church, and once there, would be offered papal protection.

But who am I to interfere with conspiratorial speculation concerning the complex American raft of church and state and its so-called separation. Yet are we not all products of sin and shame until truly born again by true repentance? Remember, there will be no sanctuary in hell for those seeking escape or solace from those everlasting fires that will never be quenched. Then, time and its significance will be worthless for the unsaved with no prospects of redemption, and instant pain relief will be denied. How shocking for all sinners to share and weep over as they contemplate what might have been!

As I write this, I am listening to the heart-wrenching final movement of the Pathetique symphony by Tchaikovsky, and somehow it brought to mind a sad story I heard some years ago.

For several years, a famous author had been nursing her husband, who was suffering from a motor neurone disease. He had been lapsing into semi-delirious moods for several days.

Then, opening his eyes one morning, he looked at his wife in a strange way and said as a matter of fact, "You know, I never loved you." The couple had been married for over thirty years. He then added, "I really only ever loved her," he whispered quietly and closed his eyes. His wife had no idea of whom he was referring to, but the pain of these words was deeply wounding for her. Later, he slipped into a coma and never recovered. I felt for his poor wife hearing these cutting words from the man that she had loved and cared for and assumed he had reciprocated her love as well, but apparently not. How turbulent her emotions must have been from that day onward as this wife prepared for her husband's funeral and entered a new era of her life!

This will happen one day, you know, at the Great White Throne Judgment when billions will cry to the Lord with excuses such as, "we prayed all the novenas, recited our rosaries, journeyed on pilgrimages to Croagh Patrick (barefoot), to Walsingham (barefoot), to Lourdes and Fatima." The Muslims will wail and insist that they visited Mecca once in their lifetime and benefited from the Quran, Buddhists will lament that they sought foolishly nirvana through yoga. All useless good works, of course, that will save nobody! Only faith in the precious blood of Jesus Christ "cleanseth us from all sin" (1 John 1:7), and "without shedding of blood is no remission (Hebrews 9:22).

However, on May 11th 1865, the unprepared prisoners were now brought up from their cells and seen blinking at the blinding sunlight in the stifling room. Then, the suffocating hoods were pulled from their heads. They were then ordered to be seated. Seated before them, it seems, and in full uniform were nine stern and unsmiling bearded military judges. They would now sit and pontificate for six sweltering weeks and mull over the evidence presented to them. With over 300 nervous witnesses to be summoned, this court apparently meant business. Occasionally, the author of "Ben Hur" General Lew Wallace would sometimes offer a faint smile at what he learnt. However, as this coordinated trial commenced, it seems most of these military men's minds considered the true culprit of the murder of their commander-in-chief to be that traitor Jefferson Davis. Naturally, Stanton would make sure they were briefed about Davis and his complicity to bring down the true government of the United States, Davis being aided in this act of treason by many other carpetbaggers and others in this Confederate mix, according to Stanton.

The eight suspected prisoners now entered the trial room in the newly "created courtroom on the third floor". The night before, the eight had heard the serious charges read to them for the first time. The canvas hoods were then removed and some had requested that the charges be read to them. The reading of the words would have been difficult to decipher by flickering candlelight. Now in the courtroom, the men, with those canvas hoods previously pulled roughly off their heads, stood and waited. They perhaps were now also suffering the discomfort of swollen and blistered feet, previously enclosed for hours in sharp foot chains.

Interestingly, Edwin Stanton had said rather optimistically that, "It was his intention that the criminals should be tried and executed before President Lincoln was buried." So, you can see his impatience to have this matter settled and sealed, hoping for the prisoners to be swinging at the end of a rope, and not before much time. It was not to be, of course. Stanton did not get his way this time.

In the open stifling court, all of the accused were seated close to each other. In a pen-and-ink drawing from the time, the accused were seen sitting tightly together on a raised wooden platform, with a five-foot rail secured in front of them. Several armed soldiers stood nearby. Mrs Mary Surratt was seen in a long black dress with a heavy veil shielding her face, perhaps from all the suspicious and sniggering spectators who had been admitted to the court. Later, for some reason, she was allowed to step down from the others and be seated next to her lawyer's table.

More favourable treatment for this lady, it seems, and just possibly because of her medical condition, it has been suggested. All pled not guilty, with the obvious failure of any methods of torture previously perpetrated on the suspects in prison to attempt to extract a guilty plea from each of them. Out of the eight prisoners, Edmond Spangler for some unknown reason has been previously subjected to the worst treatment of all the eight, it seems, being secured in rusting chains and hooded in the cramped stinking hull of the Saugus ship. There we learn: "He stands in stagnant seawater up to his waist". But, I ask, why him?

We should also mention Major Thomas Eckert, Chief of the War Department's telegraph office who had declined an invitation to join the Lincolns at the Ford Theatre as did

Ulysses Grant, and the Speaker of the House Schuyler Colfax who later became Vice President serving under President Grant. I find it all very suspicious, as I wonder about these men's motives. Thomas Eckert did accompany Edwin Stanton to the Peterson house where the dying Lincoln lay. I believe he entered that crowded bedroom with Stanton and looked upon the dying president's parched face in shock. Later, Eckert would spend hours interviewing Lewis Payne privately in a prison cell, even bringing him a wad of tobacco to chew through his canvas hood.

Apparently years later, "Eckert never revealed what he knew about the Lincoln assassination." So, I can only speculate on whether he was perhaps related in some way to Lewis Payne. Or was this act just a kind gesture or was the tobacco laced with something? Why was Payne selected for these "kind" prison chats by Eckert and what was he hoping to learn from Payne about John Wilkes Booth? It seems many other suspects had been hauled in and now numbered over three hundred swept up in this presidential playlet, being housed and detained elsewhere, of them in a pitiful and confused condition. It should be remembered also that when the noose was about to be placed around Lewis Payne's neck on the gallows, he was quoted as saying quietly, "They ain't caught half of us yet." Very strange final words from a condemned man whom I suggest knew a lot more about the other conspirators who somehow escaped Stanton's wrath.

He also said that, "Mrs Surratt is innocent. She doesn't deserve to die with the rest of us." I can't help suggesting that Payne was a mass of contradictions, but just maybe he did indeed know something important that Eckert wanted to know about.

However, back in the courtroom, permission was now gratefully given for the four windows of the courtroom to be opened. Little lost boy David Herold, who some claimed to have the mind of a 12-year-old boy, would look desolately out of the window and probably wondered why he was even there.

Lewis Powell would stare back defiantly at the gapers in the court. He seemed not to care and seemingly showed no emotions at all. Powell had incidentally been wounded at Gettysburg and may have suffered some form of head trauma because of this. No electric fans in those days, of course! And it seems also that twenty tall spittoons stood like sentries around the room. Mary Surratt would make full use of the offered palm fan now clasped tightly in her gloved hand. But what a cast of characters, it seems, wandered freely in and out of that courtroom, viewing the proceedings as a popular staged play, perhaps with refreshments being served during the court recess in and outside the stockade.

For some reason, the fair ladies of Washington had heard or seen the newspaper pictures of Lewis Payne and he seems to have made quite a stir to many of them. Hearts were fluttering, I believe, with perhaps some scented love letters being passed to his attorney. Yet, at 6'2 tall and weighing 170 lbs, he seemed uninterested and blasé about what is happening around him. Even enquiring autograph hunters would wander into the court unopposed, clutching leather-bound autograph books. Then it seems some of the judges, can you believe, we're happy to oblige the request with a signature and dedication to the owner.

I cannot confirm if any of the co-conspirators were approached or if indeed they accepted the offer to sign the book, but who knows? Some of the other Washington elite travelled into the courtroom to observe history take place, among them, bishop Simpson who would later preach at Lincoln's funeral in Springfield.

Also paying visits (out of curiosity, I suspect) were General Ulysses, Grant a future president no less, and the soldier who had declined an offer to accompany his commander-in-chief to the Ford Theatre that night.

John Hay put in an appearance, he being Lincoln's private secretary. Ward Hill Layman, he being Lincoln's self-appointed bodyguard who later purchased the funeral railcar that took Lincoln's remains to Springfield. Edwin Thomas Booth, he being John Wilkes Booth's actor brother, put in an appearance and probably would certainly have happily signed autographs. Apparently, when his brother John Wilkes Booth entered the Ford Theatre that night to shoot the president, he had spoken to several fans that recognised him and he might even have signed autographs, as he was known to do.

Concerning brother Edwin, by a strange twist of fate, he had previously saved Robert Lincoln, the president's eldest son, from death or serious injury on a railway station platform in New York. "So, it seems, one Booth brother took a Lincoln's life whilst the other saved a Lincoln's life some 20 years earlier."

Surprisingly, the 12-year-old Tad Lincoln was seen at the trial and maybe Captain Robert Lincoln, his older brother, probably both together. But Mrs Lincoln did not, it seems, make an expected appearance.

As for the rest of the crowd there, well, they just wandered in to stare, sneer and gawp at the eight accused, joined of course by the usual souvenir hunters. To them, it was just another day's entertainment, and free of charge at that.

Again we don't know if any of the pitiful prisoners on display actually signed an offered autograph book, probably not, especially as they were handcuffed, except for Mrs Surratt whose hands were free. She may well have been offered rosary beads, not that it did her any good, of course, nor will it to any other sinner who seeks solace through those worthless and wicked beads. Only true repentance and faith alone in Christ can do that.

I can't help speculating that watching these proceedings from a concealed area through a magnified viewing lens hidden in a wooden panel was good old Edwin Stanton. Now he must be obviously relishing the prisoners' discomfort and dismay of what is being offered to the court and what he can observe. Did he perhaps delight in what they had endured previously in their cells and would he be at their expected execution? Well, I suspect he was indeed there, waiting and watching as the four hung and swung from a twirling rope and smiling at what he had achieved, and all of course for his dead president's lasting legacy and his own vanity, of course. This, he must have reasoned in his attorney's brilliant mind, was what it was all about – vengeance – and as simple as that.

It also seems odd from a legal perspective that there was only one witness to the drama at the theatre and seated in the box that evening next to the wounded president, namely, Major Henry Rathbone. When he was called to offer his evidence, it seemed as if he had learned it from a prepared script, someone later remembered. Again, why wasn't the brave major's fiancée Miss Clara Harris, the daughter of New York Senator Ira Harris, called to describe to the court what she had seen? And what of Mrs Mary Todd Lincoln, you may ask. Both of these women had lived and suffered through the terror of that night at the theatre, but they were not summoned, or perhaps both declined the offer to attend. All very strange and yet I also have to speculate that Mrs Lincoln would have insisted and demanded to give her side of the story about her husband's murder, but it seemed not.

Young Fanny Steward submitted her evidence to the court, but I'm sure she would not have had the courage to enter that room and see again her father's assailant, Lewis Powell, staring at her. There were rumours that John Wilkes Booth had previously made the acquaintance of a young chambermaid in the Seward household, even giving her a diamond pin as a gift. Was this perhaps for important information concerning the layout of the house and bedroom of Secretary of State William H. Seward? Lewis Payne certainly seemed to know his way up the stairs when he attempted to murder Seward in his sick bed.

Yet, I did read that Payne had requested genuine forgiveness from the family for what he had subjected them to that terrible night, especially to young Fanny. Later, other prepped and paid prosecution witnesses would appear and disappear after giving their sometimes faulty evidence. The final outcome, of course, was always going to be a guilty verdict for the eight defendants then struggling to breathe in that hot sticky makeshift courtroom over many long weeks, always (it seems to me) with the old 'puppet master' Edwin Stanton himself pulling all the political strings covertly behind the scenes. It was indeed a strange and unreal occasion being played out in that room in 1865 about which the world has still not grasped the meaning and probably never will.

Interestingly "except for two witnesses, there was no case against Mrs Mary Surratt." But then into the picture entered John M. Lloyd, her alcoholic tenant and former Washington policeman employed at the Surrattsville tavern. The other was a paid boarder in her own home, he being Louis J. Weichmann who apparently "suffered from an inferiority complex and jealousy." They both were now secure in the prosecutor's camp and it was not looking good for the widow at this stage of the trial, as their evidence built up against her.

Of course, that suspect tavern (still standing) doubled as a sub-post office managed and operated by John Surratt, Mary's son. He had earlier been accused of receiving coded messages in the post from Confederate spies. Later, he would be unmasked and sacked. Now, I suspect Colonel Lafayette Baker who had replaced Alan Pinkerton knew of these treasonable actions the young John Surratt was performing. In fact, I would be very surprised if he did not use all of this gained information for his own purposes to arrest the Surratt family.

Louis J. Weichmann incidentally had been a failed catholic seminarian. He also had a brother who was a catholic priest. With John Surratt Jr, the two had attended the same catholic seminary, so there was a bond of friendship forged with these two young men. Later, he certainly stayed at Mrs Surratt's guesthouse in Washington (and yes, it's still standing today but is now known a popular Chinese restaurant specialising in crispy duck and chow mien and 'wok and roll').

The notorious Surratt boardinghouse now a restaurant

Of course, Weichmann had witnessed John Wilkes Booth's frequent visits to the house and knew of the private conversations that Booth shared with Mrs Surratt. "Weichmann felt left out, worst of all when they had asked him to leave the room," on several occasions, it is reported. He also coincidently was employed at the time at the War Department in Washington and may have been employed as an information-gatherer by its boss Edwin Stanton. Interestingly, after the trial, he was quickly promoted by Stanton to the Philadelphia customs house, a job for life, it seems, "but he was definitely Edwin Stanton's prosecution star witness," claims one historian, who may well be correct in this assumption.

He had certainly informed his superior at the War Department of the failed kidnapping of the president in February. Also "Doctor Mudd had been identified by Weichmann as being seen with Booth," so his evidence certainly did not help the accused. Naturally, there were other paid and bribed government witnesses lined up for the prosecution who played their part as well.

So, was Weichmann "Stanton's poodle" as he was later called? Or was he simply a "patsy" or a patriot, a perjurer, a fool or a felon in this matter? In fact, Edwin Stanton had five of the nine conspirators in prison three days after the assassination, so he had moved quickly and successfully. Nothing complicated about that! But it seems history is still judging Louis J. Weichmann for what he did and said at the trial under oath. Many details have been written and still are, of course, about this so-called miscarriage of American justice. I have highlighted only some of the salient points of interest in this book. I leave it to the reader to continue their further interest into this fascinating subject of the trial and its repercussions if they so wish.

At long last, the expected verdict was to be announced. Now I do perhaps wonder if the prisoners were cognisant of what the court's sentence had in store for each of them as they sat waiting and maybe prayed and wept in their cells. It would have been a long night for all of them, as they pondered their legal and eternal destiny.

Yet each of us will spend eternity in one of two permanent places, that is heaven or hell.

The Lord Jesus knew where He would spend eternity. He said: "I go to him that sent me." The apostle Paul had no doubt where he would spend eternity: "Having a desire to depart, and to be with Christ; which is far better" (Philippians 1:23).

So, heaven or hell, the choice is always yours. Do not delay.

Chapter 5: "The Verdict And The Aftermath"

At 11.00 am on July 6th 1865, the fate of the eight accused co-conspirators were brought by a horseback rider to the old arsenal prison in four sealed envelopes from Edwin Stanton's war department.

It was not encouraging news for the frightened and waiting accused: the following day, Mrs Mary Surratt, a Catholic, would hang; Lewis Powell/Payne, the son of a Baptist preacher, would hang; David Herold, an Episcopalian, would hang; and George Atzerodt, a Lutheran and "a cartoon of an assassin" as remembered rather unkindly by one lawyer, would also have an appointment with the hangman's rope, this being an appointment they all had hoped to avoid. But it was not to be.

The other four deluded defendants were Mudd, O'Laughlan and Arnold (sentenced to life imprisonment) and Spangler sentenced to six years. I suppose this was expected by the three, although Samuel Mudd must have expected the rope due to his personal association with John Wilkes Booth.

Apparently, there is no official record of how the nine military judges voted. Yet "the speed with which the alleged conspirators were arrested, tried and convicted, and the sentence carried out was truly breathtaking," writes Robert K. Summers.

Mary Surratt had not been offered a favourable press whilst confined in the "pen," it seems, although I do not think she was able to read any of the press comments about herself during her trial. Yet her daughter Anna certainly would have heard and read the damning news coverage of her "infamous" mother and probably had also informed her of what was being reported about the trial and its accused during her frequent visits to the prison.

One eager and spiteful journalist had referred to Mary Surratt as an "Amazon," although she was actually only 5'4 tall. Then there were cruel and mean descriptions of her black eyes and small mouth also added to this malicious mix. In other words, a "criminal's face of a cold and beguiling woman," recorded one toothless drunken hack of the lady's facial features. Oh my, the cruelty of the media even then!

Concerning John Wilkes Booth's romantic influence upon Mrs Surratt and others, it seems: "She was charmed and probably in love poor woman at the dangerous age in her sex, probably revelling in amorous fancies with this Apollo, twenty years her junior," suggested historian Lloyd Lewis. Well, maybe love or infatuation is blind, say the poets and the wise men, whoever they are, but the love of Christ for His saints is endless and always will be.

Public opinion, it seems, was never going to be in Mrs Surratt's favour prior to her hanging. Later, the written memories of the official hangman, Captain Christian Rath, stated that he believed she would never hang. Well, he got that wrong, didn't he? Incidentally, you can actually see him in those atmospheric pictures of the execution, he being seen in a white coat.

As mentioned before, public opinion during the trial was very much against Mary Surratt, but this would later turn dramatically to her favour after the verdict, with many later coming to see her as a sacrificial lamb of the Stanton establishment. Yet her local neighbours recall that when President Lincoln was murdered, her house at 604 H Street did not display the traditional black bunting usually draped over the exterior gables. Others also remembered that there was no sound of musical celebration emanating from her abode when General Lee finally surrendered his exhausted southern troops. So, it seems there would be no weeping or wailing for this Washington widow from her hostile neighbours and others the lady knew and may have socialised with for afternoon tea. Mary Surratt, of course, was the first woman ever executed by the U.S. federal government, although five of the nine sitting judges apparently sought to have Mrs Surratt's sentence commuted to serving life in prison "given her age and gender," it was later revealed. Sadly, this would offer no concerning comfort to her desperate darling daughter Anna, so plagued with grief and unhappiness.

Once the severity of her sentence had finally dawned on her, Mary Surratt sought even more comfort from her visiting priests. However, they didn't seem able to offer the lady any spiritual sustenance on her final night on earth, if we are to believe her weeping continually heard in her cell that night. More seriously, these priests must have known and colluded with their catholic hierarchy in concealing the secret whereabouts of her wanted son, John Jr. He was, I expect, making furtive plans for a fast getaway to Catholic Europe. She always had the full love and assistance of her faithful "but impressionable" daughter Anna who had been herself swept up in the numerous arrests at the Surratt boardinghouse on the night of April 17th. (Anna would herself later be released on May 11th. I'm not sure she ever fully recovered from this period in prison).

With the terrible news of her mother's hanging due in a matter of hours and now desperately alone, she turned to the president for mercy for her mother's life. I'm not sure if Fredrick Aitkin accompanied her to beg for her mother's life at the White House, but it would be very much the sort of mercy dash he would be involved in with Anna. The president would, of course, refuse the crying and hysterical girl's desperate pleas. She would later be brutally escorted from the White House grounds in tears.

In Robert Redford's 2010 movie *The Conspirator*, the role of Frederick Aitkin is glamorised. Yet the locations for the film and the executions were admirable from this catholic actor/director. There was no mention whatsoever, of course, of the Jesuit connection in the film!

Some years ago I read the memoirs of an old man who had been employed as a butler at the White House for many years, as had Duke Ellington's father. He relates a story that on the anniversary of Mary Surratt's hanging, the White House staff would hear her daughter weeping pitifully and garbling her words in the numerous rooms and corridors of the mansion.

She had also been seen, it seems, silently banging on the door of what was Johnson's dressing room, naturally pleading for her mother's life as it ebbed away.

As we know, Andrew Johnson refused her request. But I can't help speculating that if it had been President Lincoln and he had been asked by another young girl for mercy he would have complied. Strangely enough, there have also been many sightings circulating over the years of a ghostly apparition of a woman in black that wanders aimlessly through the old boardinghouse that Mary Surratt owned on H Street. Anna Surratt, of course, never fully recovered from the traumatic turns that led to her mother's hanging, and her own incarceration in prison probably did not help her anxieties. Anna would be bedridden for many years before her death in 1904, aged 61.

Another innocent victim, in my opinion, would have to be the young defenceless Adeline Fanny Seward. She had desperately and bravely fought and struggled with the giant Lewis Payne, preventing him from successfully achieving the attempted murder of her father, Secretary of State, then slowly recovering in his sickbed. She also, I suggest, never fully recovered from that terrible night or its consequences that affected her damaged life. Fanny sadly died the following year aged just 21. Her mother Frances, also involved in the altercation in the house that terrible night with Lewis Powell, would die the following year, aged 59.

William H. Seward himself expired in 1872 and was buried with his beloved daughter Fanny and his wife Frances. His last words apparently were: "Love one another." Of his young daughter's premature death he recalled this as: "Great unspeakable sorrow," which left his dreams for the future "broken and destroyed forever." For the rest of his life he "preferred to turn the scarred half of his face away from the camera and pose in profile." William H. Seward would later continue to serve as Secretary of State under President Andrew Johnson, as indeed did Secretary of State Dean Rusk, holding that same political office. Rusk would serve both the Kennedy and Johnson administrations.

Strangely enough, Seward would later journey to Salt Lake City where he met Mormon leader Brigham Young whom he had known and employed years before as a young man when Young had worked in the Seward house as a jobbing carpenter.

Anna Surratt and her tragic plight becomes interesting because entering into the film *The Conspirators* is her mother's young defence lawyer, 28-year-old Fredrick Atkins. He would make an important appearance and later be a great moral support in assisting this impressible young lady through the agony of the trial. At first, Frederick Atkins had been naturally suspicious of Mrs Surratt and her motives in the Lincoln killing at the Ford Theatre. He felt he had been pressured by his superior Reverdy Johnson into mounting a proper defence for Mrs Surratt. However, in the film, this young man gradually emerges as perhaps her only legal hope of gaining any reprieve. This young soldier-turned-lawyer quickly "argued that the military commission was highly prejudicial." Well, in this assumption he was certainly correct. After all, the eight conspirators were civilians now being tried and paraded in a military courtroom, with little time given for the prisoners to confer with their defence lawyers. It seems they would not be allowed to give evidence on their behalf either. Quite simply, Edwin Stanton wanted revenge and I doubt he cared or understood how it was to be completed. Interestingly, in my three used reference books, I can find no mention of Frederick Atkins' name in the index, I wonder why!

During the movie, young Atkins' role is greatly enlarged by the paid scriptwriters. However, it seems that after Atkins had learned of the unexpected death sentence to be handed down against Mary Surratt he took it upon himself to visit the home of Judge Andrew Wylie in the middle of the night with a request for his Honour to issue a writ of habeas corpus for the lady. This the judge finally agreed to perform, offering a false hope for Atkins to pursue legally and of course for Mary Surratt now lingering at death's door. But it was not to be, with the writ later declined by President Andrew Johnson.

This widow "who was fascinated by Booth and simply carried off her feet" would, along with the others, hang the next day. President Johnson had simply doomed Mrs Surratt to the gallows and he would utter that infamous remark about the widow and her reputation: "She kept the nest where the egg was hatched." I do speculate, however, if he did indeed say these words himself, or were they perfectly penned by a paid White House spin-doctor? Some of my other favourite presidential sound bites that you might well remember are: "There will be no whitewash at the White House" from dear old "Tricky" Dick Nixon. "We have nothing to fear but fear itself," FDR. "Fake news" has to be Donald Trump, of course. "All the way with JFK," John F. Kennedy. But I won't repeat what was said about LBJ's 1964 presidential campaign slogan, and who can forget: "Honey, I forgot to duck," attributed to Ronald "the Gipper" Reagan. Finally, "Only Americans can hurt America," proclaimed by good old Ike from his favourite golf course.

"There were four to be hanged that day but because one was a woman, Christian Rath the hangman could find nobody to dig the graves. He then promised that every man would get a drink of whisky when the thing is done. Then every soldier in the regiment stepped forward." In fact, a thousand uniformed soldiers were scattered in and around the jail area for this one-off event. In the picture of the hanging they are clearly visible on the 30-foot high prison wall, and in that hot sun as well.

During the night before the hangings, the gallows were erected high in the prison yard. The continual noise of the workmen could be clearly heard by the condemned themselves. One perspiring reporter remembered that: "Through the cells of the condemned there was wailing, terrible and long. Seven sisters hid David Herold with their embraces and a nephew of sixteen had spent the night with Davy." A local preacher would be on hand to offer his services, whether required or not.

Mary Surratt would have two catholic priests with her, offering some religious comfort (which didn't seem to help her). She would also be given powerful opiates by the prison medic Dr. Porter, it seems, to calm her nerves.

Lewis Payne would have a Baptist minister from Florida, a Mr. Gillette arriving at the prison, should he so require. Some claimed he refused all religious ministering. No relatives came to comfort Powell and it seemed he needed none. The man who had hidden in a tree was now alone and needing nobody it seems.

George Atzerodt would be spiritually prepared for death by a Mr. Butler, a Lutheran minister. It seems he hunted through his Bible meanwhile for the verse, "Be sure your sin will find you out" (Numbers 32:23) of course. Not sure why he was looking for this verse.

The other four prisoners, Spangler, Mudd, Arnold and O'Laughlin, "Knowing their departure for prison would come later," waited and brooded in their cells for what was to come.

Edman/Edmund Spangler, it seems, did not learn of his coming fate for some reason, "so he wept and howled as the final hammers rang on the gallows in the yard." And "none of the reporters bothered with these four," so obviously not newsworthy to the Washington press, it seems, of their coming fate. I can only speculate as to why Edwin Stanton did not insist that all eight should hang. He certainly had that power securely in his hands. Maybe there was an element of mercy in his Masonic heart, or had he compromised in his driven desire for justice for Lincoln? It now seems these four would live, and as it turned out, three would outlive even Edwin Stanton.

The following morning with temperatures in the high 90s and stress levels of the prisoners even higher, the four condemned prisoners entered the baking prison yard (interestingly barefoot), yet hell will be hotter. Crowds were expected and many had gathered overnight to watch and enjoy the morning's entertainment. Hawkers and vendors were also seen selling glasses of mint lemonade and blueberry muffins. Some even offered homemade peg dolls of the accused with coloured balloons affixed to their wooden trays for amusement. There was a jolly carnival atmosphere at this venue of death, and the only popular entertainment missing is the organ grinder with his tethered chattering dancing monkey. The prisoners now blinked at the harsh sunlight and seemed to be shoeless to further shame them and also hinder any audacious escape. A hush descended on the yard, with all eyes on the prisoners, most naturally on Mrs Surratt it seems.

Mary Surratt was now assisted by two catholic priests, one being Jacob Walter. He would later write that he was unable to accept the proposition that "a Catholic woman would go to communion on Holy Thursday and be guilty of murder on Good Friday." He should have studied the Jesuit order! The other cleric was B. F. Widget. Many other priests were involved with the Surratt defence, and some may have been Jesuit soldiers serving their conniving church. Remember, as Charles Chiniquy would later write: "The Jesuits killed Lincoln and buried the evidence." That old ex-catholic priest knew something about his dear friend's murder, I'm sure.

George Atzerodt would be accompanied by Rev. Butler; young David Herold by Episcopalian Rev. Olds; Lewis Payne strutted alongside Rev. Gillette and Baptist minister Rev. Striker. One report claimed: "That he walked like a king about to be crowned." It's reported also that the waiting hangman whispered in his ear as the noose was placed on his neck that: "I want you to die quick." Powell replied almost jauntily saying: "You know best." So, many will be laughing and joking before they enter into the grim gates of everlasting hell from where none return, of course. The prisoners' hands and legs were now quickly bound as the prepared death sentences are read out. Nothing can now go wrong, it seems.

Some would hear Mrs Surratt whimper: "Don't let me fall; hold on."

George Atzerodt proclaimed to the crowd: "May we all meet in the other world." Sad to say, this will be unlikely unless of course, he is referring to hell.

For modesty's sake, a cotton cloth was secured around Mrs Surratt's dress so it would not fly up when her body descended towards the ground. She was attired in a plain black "bombazine" alpaca dress with a matching black bonnet set off with a thin veil. She sat on the platform shielded from the sun by a large black umbrella provided to her. This created a ghostly effect on the gathering crowd, many later remembered in regard to the events that day.

As the printed order of execution was proclaimed, Mrs Surratt was seen to kiss the crucifix offered by one of the waiting priests standing next to her. The condemned took chairs and Mrs Surratt swayed against her priest. "Then the back door opened and general Hancock strode out nodding to Rath, he orders him by saying: "Go ahead, Rath." "The hangman incredulously enquired: "Her too?" The general nodded. "The State has spoken, it seems, and it must not be disobeyed. All four would hang. There is a silent agreement, it seems, that the state must be served at all cost."

George Atzerodt would be heard to cry out: "God help me now, Oh...Oh...Oh." We say: "Believe on the Lord Jesus Christ, and thou shalt be saved" (Acts 16:31).

At 1:30 pm, the four finally dropped to their death. This moment will forever be frozen in time in Alex Gardener's iconic picture. The bodies were allowed to hang for ten minutes, then cut down, and waiting army surgeons would pronounce life extinct.

Some news reports stated that no necks were broken, but others disagreed. Yet: "The head of her who had been Mrs Mary Surratt fell broken, necked upon her breast." "She makes a good bow," chirped a bystander. It seems he would be sternly rebuked by one of the shocked soldiers for this unkind comment.

Amazingly, selfish souvenir hunters descended on the wooden gallows like flies, snatching articles to plunder. Years later, after the death of one of the hangman's helpers, four separate three-foot lengths of the ropes that served their purpose that day were discovered wrapped in an old army blanket in the trunk of the deceased, very macabre.

I can only speculate that Edwin Stanton observed this "slice of history" and relished its final outcome from the building. I also suggest he must have been delighted to see the four bodies swaying from the rope. His only possible regret was that John Wilkes Booth was not joining them on the scaffold for this reuniting of the conspirators.

Later, the bodies were taken down and fitted into the prepared coffins with their names and crimes being written out on long strips of paper, then placed in sealed glass bottles upon the bodies. Maybe this was done as a record for any future exhumations. When Lewis Payne's body was viewed years later, his printed paper prison details had been eaten away, perhaps by mites.

Strangely enough, when Lewis Payne's body was released with the other co-conspirators, his skull was found to be missing, can you believe? This was later located by chance, with the number "2244 skull of a white male" stencilled on the forehead. Obviously a "Smithsonian" museum identification number, it seems. The skull was later buried in 1994 beside Lewis Payne's late mother in a Florida cemetery. It is thought that his body lies elsewhere in a mass grave at Rock Creek off lot 23, it has been suggested. But all very strange, it seems.

George Atzerdot's final resting place is apparently unknown. It seems he had a brother serving in the Washington police who may have arranged a secret location site for when his brother's body was finally released to the family and did not want the publicity.

Those four hanged co-conspirators have now earned their place in the history books, with most of the others involved now forgotten. You know, every so often a new television special or a new book concerning the Lincoln shooting arrives to a fanfare of publicity, but I notice that they actually offer nothing of substance to the reader/viewer who specialises in this fascinating subject.

President Lincoln has taken John Wilkes Booth with him, as did JFK with Lee Harvey Oswald into the history books and the History Channel. I find it rather interesting that those past assassinators of Presidents Garfield and McKinley (these being Charles Guiteau and Leon Czolgosz) were quickly forgotten then and still are unknown today.

Today, myths are maintained and managed and possibly manipulated by media men and women and none more so than in the Lincoln legend. His sombre face adorns coins, holograms, t-shirts, coffee mugs, underwear, shoes/boots, and umbrellas, with garish dog bowls and many more items to purchase if you so wish. Even the Ford Theatre's museum today has a plastic mannequin of a scowling John Wilkes Booth about to pull that infamous trigger into the head of the commander-in-chief. But, interestingly, nothing of Lee Harvey Oswald in Dallas can be seen aiming his rifle from the Texas Book Depository Building on Elm Street toward the head of JFK in his car convoy.

The then-remaining four other prisoners sentenced in the court in 1865 were: Mudd, Spengler, O'Laughlan and Arnold. They would eventually be deported to the grim island prison of Fort Jefferson, 70 miles off Key West. It's now a tourist stop-off, I understand, for popular cruise liners.

I ought to bring to your attention another infamous doctor caught up in the Lincoln assassination and detained for three weeks as a possible serious accomplice to the crime and of great interest to the police, namely Francis Tumblety. He would later be quietly released in London, England. It is possible that

Tumblety was seen in Booth's company by Lafayette Baker's spies before the killing of Lincoln.

There may have been a future role for this doctor that would benefit Wilkes Booth in his escape after the shooting. Of course, the escape plan went terribly wrong for him, as we know, when he fell and injured his leg in the Ford Theatre. He could not, of course, have seen this calamity coming, could he? Isn't it always the little, unforeseen things that can trip you up?

Later, when domiciled in England some years later, Tumblety was seriously suspected by Scotland Yard to be "Jack the Ripper," is then responsible for five unsolved murders in the East End, some say maybe more. The escaping American doctor would later jump bail and set sail to America from France. Once there, he would have to be kept under surveillance by the New York Police acting with the Yard. Now it gets interesting because, after the doctor's death in 1903, some macabre anatomy parts were discovered in his personal possessions, along with small rings, some English money and other useless female trinkets. These may well, of course, have been the missing body parts and personal property of the five unfortunate women murdered in Whitechapel, London, in 1888-1891.

These grisly murders were never solved possibly due to political reasons!

The final curtain must slowly descend at last on this American tragedy. Yet out of the shed blood of the US Civil War, a country was united perhaps reluctantly and still is just about being held together today. But at a terrible personal price, it seems, with maybe a million killed, maimed and largely forgotten. In fact, many Confederate statues of Jefferson Davis, General Robert E. Lee and other heroes of the South are today being quietly removed or torn down with little or no objection, it seems, from the public.

At his second inauguration, President Abraham Lincoln quoted Matthew 18:7: "Woe unto the world because of offences! for it must needs be that offences come, but woe to that man by whom the offence cometh!"

Later he would proclaim on the steps of the White House that with: "Malice towards none, with charity for all, with firmness in the right as God gives to us to see the right." A month later Abraham Lincoln was assassinated.

On a personal note, when I came across James Swanson's book by chance, I could not have foreseen that it would occupy six months of my life in researching, examining and writing this book on Abraham Lincoln. Like Hemmingway always reminded writing "scribes" to "be there," I have tried to heed and practice his advice by immersing myself in that volatile but fascinating period of American history.

It's almost as if John Wilkes Booth, Mrs Surratt, Edwin Stanton, David Herold, Dr. Mudd, Lewis Payne, Ed Spangler, Sam Arnold, as well as young Fanny Seward and the distraught Anna Surratt, with many more, of course, seemed to have taken up a *permanent occupation* in my daily life, but they must now take their leave of me. I have even dreamed about some of them! Can you believe? How sad, I know! All have since departed into their waiting graves long ago and far away. I suspect many are unsaved, now awaiting their own prepared judgment as explained in Revelation 20:12 of which I now quote: "And I saw the dead, small and great, stand before God; and the books were opened: and another book was opened, which is *the book* of life: and the dead were judged out of those things which were written in the books, according to their works."

So, finally, dear reader, it is not with reluctance that I happily bid them all a lasting adieu.

Epilogue

The Judah Benjamin/Rothschild/Jesuit/Bank of Montreal is still a crucial connection in the assassination that has never been fully explained and probably never will be.

But what of the audacious "Dahlgren" fiasco perhaps dreamed up by Edwin Stanton himself, when a one-legged Colonel Ulric Dahlgren with a selected force of troops was hopefully to liberate hundreds of captured Union troops, then with anticipation march on to Richmond. "Once in the city it must be destroyed, and Jefferson Davis and cabinet killed." These were apparently the sealed orders entrusted to the colonel and found in his uniform. Of course, none of it happened, with the ill-fated Colonel Dahlgren later being killed in action at age 21 by Confederate troops. Apparently, there was a disgraceful display of his corpse in Richmond for several weeks. This naturally inflamed the North.

Afterwards, rumours suspiciously emerged that the War Department plans on the Richmond sacking and Jefferson's cabinet assassination that were discovered on Dahlgren's body had been forged by the Confederates, can you believe? Today it is difficult to elucidate the truth of this military debacle of 1864. But more importantly, did this fuel the future attempt to assassinate President Lincoln, perhaps as a reprisal, and maybe on personal orders from Jefferson Davis himself to kill Lincoln?

Davis was very close to the Vatican, it seems, and even received a letter delivered to him in prison at Fort Monroe by a catholic priest dispatched from Pope Pius IX himself, with the gift of a miniature woven crown of thorns and 'blessed' by the old boy himself, I suppose. A Biblical text was also thrown in, that being Matthew 27:29, for Davis to read.

This crown of thorns was sent to Jefferson Davis by Pope Pius IX in sympathy for Davis' post war treatment by the US government while a prisoner at Fortress Monroe.

It seems that Mrs Mary Todd Lincoln sadly descended into a slow mental state of decline after departing Washington. Her son Tad had died in 1871 before he reached manhood. His mother would later attend and arrange séances in the false hope of communicating with her late husband, her two sons, and her brother. She also suffered from hallucinations and feared for her life. So much so that her son Robert had her committed to a private insane asylum, from which she somehow escaped. In her twilight years, "she shut herself away in a darkened room, preferring candlelight to sunlight." She died in 1882 "pitifully in her sister's home at Springfield, after years of insanity."

Laura Keene (the actress, producer and theatre manager) died in 1873 from tuberculosis, she was 47. In spite of those cruel critics claiming she offered no comfort to the dying president (and why wasn't his own wife cradling his head, you may ask, certainly a valid question), Dr. Teale's autobiography does confirm Laura's compassionate actions that fateful night. And that's good enough for me.

Robert Lincoln, the only surviving son of the Lincolns, later held the office of Secretary of War. He would witness two other presidential assassinations, these being Garfield and McKinley. He also served as the US Ambassador to London. He died in 1922 and is buried in Arlington National Cemetery.

Edwin M. Stanton died in 1869, he was just 55. He had been involved with the important impeachment of President Johnson. President Grant had later nominated him for the Supreme Court but died before he could take up that appointment. There was an unconfirmed rumour that he had committed suicide, but I doubt that he would have even considered this. It was just not his style, and he certainly wasn't a coward. He is buried in the Oak Hill Cemetery in Georgetown; "few people visit his grave," writes James Swanson. But if I ever get to visit Washington I will certainly make a point to call and pay my respects and leave some of our own Bible ministry tracts at the graveside. This was the man Lincoln had defended so often during the Civil War. Yet in that boardinghouse, as he watched over the dying president "he was now dictator," which none can deny. All of his previous loathing for Lincoln now seems to have turned to love. All these deeds after the shooting of Lincoln are, I believe, unparalleled in American history.

Doctor Charles Leale died in 1932 at the age of 90.

Major Henry Rathbone and Clara Harris were married and had a family. However, on 23rd December in 1883 after acting strangely "Rathbone attempted to murder his children, when a nurse intervened he shot his wife then stabbed her to death. He would later try to commit suicide himself. He would somehow escape from America "but spent the rest of his years in a German asylum."

Maybe it would have been better for "Clara if Wilkes Booth had stabbed her fiancé and slain him in the Ford Theatre in 1865," writes James Swanson. Cynical, but true.

For Boston Corbett, the man who supposedly shot Wilkes Booth at Garrett's Farm, fame lasted a short time. He later took a job as an assistant doorkeeper in the Kansas House of Representatives. "One morning he appeared with revolvers in each hand and opened fire on the legislators and the ladies. Overpowered he was committed to an insane asylum but escaped." It is rumoured but not confirmed that he is buried in Enid, Oklahoma.

John M. Lloyd, the star witness against Mary Surratt, died from alcoholic poisoning.

Christian Rath, the hangman, many years later would recall that: "The hanging gave me a lot of trouble. I took Mrs Surratt's body down from the gallows and placed it in the coffin." He died in 1920.

Suicides within the year would claim the lives of the two senators - King and Lane - who both cruelly prevented Anne Surratt from appealing personally to President Johnson for her mother's reprieve.

Louis Weichmann faced open hostility for his part in testifying against Mary Surratt. He later operated a business academy and died in 1902. He never recanted of what he had informed the court, concerning what he had heard Booth and Surratt discussing privately in her boardinghouse. In recording the cause of death, his doctor had written, "extreme nervousness."

John Surratt fled to the open arms of the Vatican just hours after the shooting of Lincoln. Once there, he enlisted and became "a papal Zouaves wearing the colourful effeminate uniform of the army of the papal state." He would, it seems, be housed at the English College in Rome, this being where the formation of "elite" catholic priests are trained then and today. It's interesting that he did not lodge at the Pontifical North American College where the training of American men for the priesthood usually takes place. I do wonder what the English connection here was.

Surratt would later be returned to the United States and there stand trial twice in a civil court and not a military one. All charges were conveniently dismissed against him through the legal statutes of limitations. He would later tread the lecture circuit, but audiences turned against him and John Surratt never lectured again.

This former catholic seminarian died in 1916 taking those secrets of Wilkes Booth and himself to the grave. He would almost certainly have hanged in 1865 and possibly with his mother if Edwin Stanton's soldiers had captured him alive. I do suggest that those years afterwards allowed him to prepare his answers when asked of his own important role with Wilkes Booth, obviously minimising his own crucial role in the murder of the president. Another man who had the rare opportunity of preparing his answers for the media and of his own actions pre the Second World War was Sir Oswald Mosley.

Somewhere in all of this conspiracy is the hand of "the Saint Leopold foundation," a secret Jesuit spy network. Also, the "Sulpician Fathers" cannot be ignored; apparently they "sprang out of a Jesuit root." Their order had a motherhouse in Montreal, it seems, operating at the time of the assassination of Lincoln. Both Surratt and Weichmann studied and visited there, it is claimed. All very suspicious!

William Peterson, the proprietor of the boardinghouse where Lincoln expired, committed suicide by swallowing laudanum!

Samuel Arnold survived the prison island's harsh regime at Fort Jefferson. After his release, he would author his own memoirs and die in 1902.

Michael O'Laughlin would die of yellow fever on the same island, being nursed at the end by doctor Mudd.

Ned Spangler would be released from the Island in 1869. He had formed a close bond with Mudd and later died on Mudd's farm in 1875.

Samuel Mudd would be released from Jefferson Island after his medical efforts with other doctors helped to contain the yellow fever outbreak. "Dr Mudd returned to his farm in 1869. Happy to be free of the black prison guards he despised," we read. Later both Presidents Carter and Reagan were sympathetic (for some reason) to the Mudd family's ongoing effort to clear his name.

The US Government would later purchase the Ford Theatre in 1866, to be used for storage facilities and medical records, it seems. In 1893, a floor in the building collapsed, killing 22 clerks and injuring 68 more. It's believed some of the inquest medical notes held on the "Montauk" concerning John Wilkes Booth's body and his final autopsy results "were lost in the avalanche of fire and mortar." Today it is a working museum.

"I have laboured for and not against the Union," Abraham Lincoln.

"It is appointed unto men once to die, but after this the judgment" (Hebrews 9:26).

Books and articles

The Lincoln Conspiracy, Balsiger and Sellier Jr.

Manhunt, James L. Swanson

Myths after Lincoln, Lloyd Lewis

David McGowan 1960-2015, Internet articles

P.S. It had been my intention in this series to examine the important role of President Lincoln and his relationship with the Mormons, but space and time did not allow me to complete it this time.

Also by James Battell

The Shocking History of the Jesuits (The Society of Jesus)

King James I of England: The King The Vatican Could Not Kill

The Hidden Truth About Freemasonry, The Catholic Church, And The Illuminati

Bible Prophecy Made Simple For Serious Students of Scripture

Did The Catholic Church Order Abraham Lincoln's Assassination?

Is Calvinism And The Doctrines of Grace Biblical?

The Book of Genesis Commentary (Chapters 1-11)

Watchman Nee, Witness Lee, and Living Stream Ministry: A Critical Analysis of Their Identity as Cult or Church

What Is Speaking In Tongues And Is It Still For Today?

Ephesians Bible Commentary

The Book of Romans Commentary